C000198178

voices of
Petersfield
and District

Tempus ORAL HISTORY *Series*

voices of
Petersfield
and District

Pamela Payne

TEMPUS

Sam Hardy and friends with horses and carriage.

Frontispiece: *'Three little maids are we'. Depicting the 'upstairs/downstairs' theme of this book. The girl on the right is Mary Mabel Danby, Phyllis Gilburd's mother, in 1906.*

First published 2003

Tempus Publishing Limited
The Mill, Brimscombe Port,
Stroud, Gloucestershire, GL5 2QG

www.tempus-publishing.com

© Pamela Payne, 2003

The right of Pamela Payne to be identified as the Author
of this work has been asserted by her in accordance with the
Copyrights, Designs and Patents Act 1988.

All rights reserved. No part of this book may be reprinted
or reproduced or utilised in any form or by any electronic,
mechanical or other means, now known or hereafter invented,
including photocopying and recording, or in any information
storage or retrieval system, without the permission in writing
from the Publishers.

British Library Cataloguing in Publication Data.
A catalogue record for this book is available from the British Library.

ISBN 0 7524 3127 7

Typesetting and origination by Tempus Publishing Limited
Printed in Great Britain by Midway Colour Print, Wiltshire

Contents

Acknowledgements

The main villages incorporated in this book are: Liss, Buriton, Stroud, Steep, Sheet and Harting. Several other local villages are also mentioned, such as Longmoor, East Meon and Langrish.

I am indebted to the thirty-three very special people whose memories and photographs are in this book; I am deeply grateful for their interest, enthusiasm and co-operation.

Many thanks to two friends who are Society of Women Writers and Journalists colleagues and fellow Tempus authors: Sylvia Kent, without whom this book would not have been written, and Judith Spelman for her invaluable technical advice. Thank you Jennifer Robinson and Paul Gouldstone for your recording of the Sherrington interview and June Edwards for your father's memoirs.

I am grateful for the help given by: Des Farnham and the staff of the Petersfield Library; Doreen Binks and Mary Ray of the Petersfield Museum which, should you wish to hear more oral histories, has an excellent archive of its own. Also to the Hampshire County Council Museums Service for allowing me to reproduce some of Flora Twort's paintings.

Every effort has been made to trace the copyright of all photographs. If I have accidentally infringed any copyright I apologise and would be glad to rectify this in any future edition of the book.

Loving thanks to my mother, Dorothy Allan, for her encouragement over the years and to my brother, Andrew Allan, for sorting out the computer bugs! Heartfelt and loving thanks to my husband, Roger, for reading and correcting the final drafts and putting up with my sitting in front of the dreaded machine when we could have been out enjoying the sunshine together!

Finally, I dedicate this book to my Dad.

Introduction

'Petersfield... a town eminent for little but it being full of good inns'
Daniel Defoe, 1726.

Today, the first half of Defoe's statement couldn't be further from the truth: Petersfield is most definitely pre-eminent, as witnessed by the testimonies of my contributors. However, Defoe was right about the 'good inns'; a few have been mentioned in this book and I am only sorry I was unable to include them all. Petersfield was once a staging post on the main London to Portsmouth coaching route; travellers would stop at the inns for rest and recuperation, their horses would be stabled and often a fresh team would be harnessed for the onward journey, so the inns were fundamental in Defoe's time – and are indispensable in ours!

Today, Petersfield is an ancient country town nestling in the heart of rural Hampshire with a wealth of lovely old buildings. Just a short walk from its centre is the Heath, which boasts a 22-acre recreational lake that began life as a marsh, until eighteenth-century farmers decided that it would be better to have a lake than lose their cattle to the mud! The Square is dominated by the 1753 equestrian statue of King William III and flanked by the beautiful Norman church of St Peter. It is one of the few towns in the south of England to retain its twice-weekly market, which is held on the same site as when the town was founded in the early twelfth century. The pretty satellite villages, although independent in many ways, are nevertheless an integral part of the life of Petersfield and that is why I felt compelled to include them in my book. With the Queen Elizabeth Park, South Downs Way, Sheet Common, the Hangars and Durford Wood on its doorstep, Petersfield is a haven for naturalists, walkers and riders, but most of all it is most definitely an eminent town in which to live.

Surely Defoe spent time talking to the locals in those 'good inns' he so obviously enjoyed? Did he not discover that Petersfield is steeped in the history of its colourful and often eccentric people? Did he not delight in their sense of humour, their musical, dramatic and artistic talents, their social conscience, their strongly-held political beliefs and their innate loyalty to their town or village? All these reasons and more are why the area has attracted royalty, the aristocracy, the famous and infamous and ordinary folk like you and me.

Throughout my research, the overwhelming impression of Petersfield and district in the last two centuries is one of an 'upstairs/downstairs' society. Grand houses appear to have been the main employers, each affording a microcosm of society with its own hierarchy and social structure – even the lowliest prospective employee was asked if he or she sang tenor or soprano so that the household could uphold the tradition of providing a choir for the Petersfield Musical Festival. With the possible exception of farming, other trades, although important, appeared to take second place in the employment stakes. Things changed in the mid-twentieth century when the 'Dickensian' rubber factory was the biggest employer for a time. Now we are as diverse as any other thriving and prosperous market town, with new industry and the further development of our natural resources. Happily, however, some things don't change – we continue to enjoy music, drama and the arts and, of course, we still have our market and Taro Fair!

If ever I was harbouring any doubts about the validity or usefulness of a book such as this, they were swept aside when I read the roughly-written memoirs of Harry Walter Edwards, who was born on 15 April 1904 and who died on 11 August 1980, after a long and ordinary life spent in and around Petersfield. He wrote his memoirs in 1977 but stopped when he reached 1930, as he became terminally ill. According to his daughter, June Edwards, he wrote as he spoke: poetically, humorously, evocatively and full of colour. Similarly, Jennifer Robinson, daughter of Violet and Reginald Sherrington, allowed me to step back into her late parents' world by lending me a tape of an interview (made by Paul Gouldstone for the National Trust) on the occasion of their diamond wedding anniversary. They, like Mr Edwards, had been in service in one of the many manor houses in the area; their stories, and many others in this book, exemplify life below stairs. Conversely, Charles Hardy paints a vivid picture of his late father, Squire Sam Hardy, and his 'upstairs' life; this is given credence by the tales of those who were in his employ. Whilst wishing I had been able to meet the Sherringtons, Mr Edwards and Squire Hardy, I realised that by writing this book I had the opportunity to capture the equally important memories of those still living in Petersfield and the neighbouring villages. Their reminiscences, recorded and transcribed with the minimum of editing, are just as fascinating. Some memories go as far back as Harry's, others are more recent but all are documented for future generations. Such was their enthusiasm that I was more than 20,000 words over my publisher's limit and reluctantly had to cut the text!

I finished reading Harry's memoirs in my garden on the first warm day of spring. The birds were singing, the air was filled with the scent of spring flowers and, as Harry had said, 'All things seemed to fall into its own allotted space'. Suitably inspired, I eschewed the delights of a sunny day and came in to draft this introduction – well before the book was finished. Thank you Harry, Violet, Reg and Sam for speaking to me from 'beyond'; and a very big 'thank you' to all those who generously shared their stories with me; I am greatly in your debt. I have learnt a great deal about my town and made many new friends; I just hope I have done you justice.

Pamela Payne
November 2003

1 Early Days

My birth

Some years ago Dolly Alwyn, who kept the Market Inn, told me the story of the day of my birth. Old Mr Alwyn said, 'Sam's bound to put something on – get the settee out', and they plonked it on the grass outside the house. Dolly told me: 'Mum got out the rugs and got comfy and a lot of people brought chairs. Your Dad held you out the window and nearly bloody well dropped you! – we didn't know what to do so we sang *God Save the King*. Then the doors of the house opened and kegs of beer were brought out and we all cheered and sang *God Save the King* again! My dad was crafty, he said, 'Put one of the kegs by me and I'll dish it out'. More and more people came from Petersfield and we had a real singsong, the beer flowed and it was all free!'

Charles Hardy

Born in a pub!

My paternal grandparents were Henry and Maud Sherrington and my maternal grandparents were William and Agnes Tubbs. Grandfather Sherrington ran the Greyhound pub in West Harting and my father, Reginald, was born there. They moved to South Harting in the 1930s and my father and two uncles, Roy and William Sherrington, rang the St Mary's church bells and sang in the choir. My mother, Violet, worked at Uppark as a scullery maid; it was there she met my father, Reg, the garden boy. I was born in South Harting in 1932, the second oldest of their four children. Grandfather Sherrington ran the South Harting grocery and cheese store and I would spend two weeks of my summer holidays there. He wore a lovely white starched apron and I watched him cutting the big round cheeses with a cheese wire. Aunt Florrie was the local district nurse and midwife, and Uncle Roy Sherrington was a painter and decorator who worked for Cousins, the Compton builders. One day, when he was painting the South Harting School, he fell backwards off his ladder and died. My eldest brother, Gerald, sadly died of cancer when he was only fifty-six.

Jennifer Robinson

'Sir Daddy'

I was born in 1934 in a little thatched cottage at No. 20, Bones Lane, Buriton. At that time, my father, Harry Walter Edwards, was butler and valet to Colonel Algernon Bonham-Carter at the manor house. The Colonel always called him 'Ted' and they spent a lot of time fishing together. They became close friends and he was there for thirty-odd years, until the Colonel died in 1960. I didn't see a lot of my father because he was always working and he didn't get home till late in the evening. I used to call him 'Sir'! You see he was always up at the manor and, as we always called the Colonel 'Sir', father was also 'Sir'.

Henry and Maud Sherrington.

Rose Cottage, where June Edwards lived.

When the Colonel died, father went to Durford Place as gardener. My mother, Pansy, who was from South Wales, also went into service when she was fourteen at the big Adhurst St Mary's house in Petersfield and then she went to work for Sam Hardy, which was how she met my father – he was the footman there. They were married in Wales in 1932 and had been together for over forty-seven years when father died in August 1980 at the age of seventy-six. Like most of the village, my mother sometimes worked as housemaid down at the manor and she used to do a lot of dressmaking for the Bonham-Carter girls. She also worked for Canon Morley at the rectory; she would go down and do his cooking and cleaning.

June Edwards

First motorcar

My pal Giggy Pledger and I used to go to the Petersfield pond to fish; we had 'cutty hank' lines with a big eel hook. We used to take our shoes and stockings off and wade out, sometimes standing in the water for hours. One day, in about 1910, Giggy and I heard this banging noise on the Portsmouth Road; we dried our feet, dressed and then ran along to the crossroads at the bottom of Sussex Road. We were there just in time to see this contraption coming towards the crossroads – it was a car, the first car I had ever seen. It wasn't like the ones we have today; this was a sort of box with a sloping front, a huge steering wheel, solid rubber tyres and big brass lamps that I suppose burnt paraffin. The driver wore a tweed cape and hat and a huge pair of goggles. I suppose the speed was only about 10 miles per hour; it went away up Dragon Street like a bat-out-of-hell, smoke everywhere and the police chasing it. Fantastic!

Harry Edwards (father of June)

Squire Sam Hardy

My father was a farmer but the family also had a brewery in Manchester called Hardy's Crown Brewery. It had been going since the eighteenth century and he had an income from his share. They owned a lot of pubs, all along the main road from Altrincham in Cheshire, right through into the middle of Manchester. The family were farmers in the beginning; they came down from Scotland after the 1745 rebellion and started to farm in Derbyshire. In about 1810 one member of the family went to Manchester and started the brewery. At that time Mr and Mrs Seaward of Borough House, Petersfield, owned all the land up to Weston and my father's elder brother (who was twenty years older than him and running the brewery) used to come all the way from Manchester to buy hops from the Seawards – they were the best hops going. My father wanted to learn to farm instead of going to Cambridge so his brother said, 'I'll ask Charlie Seaward whether he'll take you on and teach you farming'. That is how Sam Hardy came to Petersfield. He became a good farmer and used to take the prizes for the best butter, best milk and so on. He was mad about his farm but I was never able to find out whether it ran at a loss or not. The Seawards eventually became my godparents.

Charles Hardy

Sam Hardy.

Goodyers

We had a house in Woodbury Avenue, which had three bedrooms, but then we had three children so we thought we needed four bedrooms. We already had property in The Spain, which is now the yard to the west of us, and we were in the process of buying the stable block from the owners of Goodyers when Alan said, 'They want to sell the house now, come and see it'. We fell in love with Goodyers and made an offer, which was accepted. Nonie was born there and Hillary arrived later so we ended up with five children! The house was named after John Goodyer, the seventeenth-century botanist and herbalist. He came from a farming family and had had legal training and was therefore a very good estate administrator. He was working for Bishop Bilson's family when Thomas Bilson (the Bishop's son) of Mapledurham House gave him the house and land, for special services. When Goodyer died he left his library of books and papers to Magdalen College, Oxford, and bequeathed the house and some land to form the Weston Charity – 'To put forth the young of the tithing of Weston' – which still continues its good work today by helping local schools and impoverished students.

Mary Ray

1924 wedding

My parent's wedding was in 1924 and the road leading to Steep church was decorated with beautiful spring flowers – hyacinths, daffodils and God knows what else – in December! They were sent in a refrigerated train from the south of France and popped in place on the morning of the wedding. The honeymoon was to have been in the south of France but father said, 'I'm Master of Hounds and it clashes with the hunting, so I thought we'd have three nights at the Savoy and go back to Petersfield; after all, Petersfield is much better than the south of France!'.

Charles Hardy

Synagogue

When I married Ken, a BOAC pilot, we lived abroad for ten years. Sir Bernard Burrows, who was the Resident of Bahrain, heard that we were going back to England and said, 'Where are you going to live?' We had no idea, but thought it ought to be quite near the London airport. And so he said, 'You know, Petersfield is quite a good place, it's a halfway house and I've got a cottage at Steep Farm – perhaps you would like to live there until you

find something?' We have never left Petersfield since then! Our son was already in a boarding school but our daughter went right the way through Bedales. We have always lived in the same house, apart from Sir Bernard's cottage. Dear John Dowler, a prominent estate agent, looked at this house and said 'Oh my goodness, no! The foundations are sinking and it's an old building, but I'll offer them £3,500' – which was quite a lot of money then. It was owned by a Mr Levy, who owned the company, Itside Rubber, which gave employment to a lot of Petersfield people in those days. The family were Jewish and the sitting room was where they prayed on a Saturday; the house was their home but it also acted as a synagogue. The postman used to bring the food because they were not allowed to do anything on the Sabbath – they were very religious. Some members of the Levy family have come to visit us, just to see the place where they were born. It had a very sombre sitting room with Lincrusta all round and everything was very dark and rather eerie. Once the house was ours we decorated it and turned it into a normal living room.

Elsa Bulmer

The poor house

I was born in Buriton in 1929 in a house that was, and still is, called the Poor House. There were six cottages altogether in those days but now there are just four, and all are nice private houses. In 1991 the people that lived there organised a buffet lunch for all the people who had lived in the six houses and we were able see them as they are now. It was a nice sunny day and the lunch was outside in the courtyard. It was a very nice thing to do.

Sheila Alder

The wedding of Sam and Ruth Hardy. Petersfield's gentry all attended the squire's wedding.

The Poor House, Buriton, c. 1980, birthplace of Sheila Alder.

A gift!

My father was Master of Hambledon Hounds. He kept the hounds up the Causeway next to the Jolly Sailor public house. He owned a building opposite the kennels which had just an enormous shower room and a big dressing room where he kept all his hunting clothes; he would be filthy from hunting so he would wash and change up there before coming home. Just before the war he gave up hunting and somebody said that they didn't have a house so father said, 'I never use this place now, do you want it?' 'Oh thank you very much, Mr Hardy', came the reply and so he gave it to them – it must be worth about £200,000 now! He was very generous; even though he lost his money in the 1929 crash, his will decreed that I should continue giving whisky and coal to the poor!

Charles Hardy

Buriton Manor

We children used to go to the Buriton Manor dairy to collect our milk; we had metal cans with lids on and we used have competitions where we would swing the cans in a circle without the milk spilling out – some of us failed and had to go back for more milk! At Christmas time there would be a party for the children of the farm workers and we'd all have a little gift. We would also go up to

Two views of Buriton Manor.

Buriton House, which was the other big house in the village. Colonel Bonham-Carter had three daughters, Pansy, Marigold and Daphne, and when they all were presented at Court, father went with them to Buckingham Palace. He also attended each of their weddings. Admiral Stuart Bonham-Carter used to live by the Heath in Petersfield and when he came to see the Colonel he would bring his daughter Joanna, who is roughly the same age as me, and we played together in the manor.

Father used to say that Buriton Manor was haunted because he often heard footsteps on the gravel walks that went round the house, especially on bright moonlit nights, but there was never anyone there. Mother often helped out when they had dinners and I used to sleep in a room that had a sloping floor. It had a most uncanny feel to it – nobody told me at the time but it was supposed to be haunted. There was a blocked passageway in the cellars that led from the manor to the church and then to the old rectory. Cromwell visited the manor and Edward Gibbon lived there. It had huge flagged floors and old wood, which smelled so good. I should remember more about the manor because I once won a competition at school for writing a history about it.

June Edwards

Victorian railway

There used to be a nice Victorian railway station in Liss but that was all modernised; the signal box went as well as the lovely wooden gates – the signalman used to wind them open. It was much prettier and we used to have a little newspaper stall. I used to travel to Longmoor on the train, which was called the Bullet. I would take my bicycle to Liss and one of the small shops used to let me leave it round the back. The Bullet was just for the soldiers and people who worked at Longmoor; the soldiers would use it to get to the mainline station before going home on leave. The Longmoor line has gone and it is now the Riverside Walk.

Jennifer Robinson

Ramshill railway bridge

When the Petersfield to Midhurst railway line was finished, the old bridge had to be demolished, so there was great excitement because the army was going to do it at midnight. We all turned out to watch, with great expectations. They pressed the plunger but only part of the structure came down so they had to do it again the next night. We didn't bother going – it was all a bit of an anti-climax.

John Freeman

Surgery

The *Petersfield Herald* office used to be Dr Peter's house. We would go down the little alleyway alongside the house, ring the doorbell and be let into the yard behind, where his surgery was, and do you know, that bit of Petersfield is still the same as when I went to the doctor's at five years old! I can't believe that it hasn't been touched; everything else in Petersfield has changed. We used to ring the bell and two smart ladies would come, and one was my cousin, Lottie Tipper (she married Ern Berryman, the butcher in West Liss); she was the cook and Mrs Fiander, from up Cranford Road, was house parlour maid. Mrs Peters and her daughter used to teach music and play the piano and violin for all the functions in the town.

Nancy de Combe

Nancy de Combe.

Broke my collarbone

The surgery was at Winton House, down the little footpath going towards the Folly Market. I went there when I fell off a gate and broke my collarbone. It hurt so much that I ran out of the surgery with just a pair of knickers on and my arm in a sling – my mother had to chase me all down the High Street! They then moved the surgery to the old post office that was at the bottom of the High Street. The doctors there were Dr Pankridge, Dr Cross (who'd lost a leg), Dr Jeffreys, Dr Cook, and Dr Hooey. Dr Pankridge used to ride his horse up The Causeway to go to Buriton to see his patients – outside of our place we had a ring on the wall and he used to tie his horse up and come in and have a cup of tea and something to eat and see if we were all alright.

Nancy Ford

Kimber's zoo

Mr Kimber was a well-known local character. He used to sell newspapers on the corner of The Square, by Lloyds Bank, but he also had a zoo on his land up at Tilmore. He kept wild animals in cages on wheels – tigers, monkeys, cheetahs and so on – two of each. It was a business; he used to sell them to zoos and the circus. One day a tiger got out and frightened people, though it was eventually caught. Some of the monkeys used to get out as well. It must have been awful for the people who lived round there, to hear these lions roaring at night. It would never be allowed now. He was very kind to people though; he used to buy the papers back off you – for recycling!

John Freeman

Biggest rats in the world!

I've still got the last gates from Mr Kimber's lion cage; his son Geoff, who is now dead, gave them to me. I would play football with Geoff and he used to show me the various animals. One day he had a big chicken coop filled with coypus (they used to call them the biggest rats in the world). They had been found in the Liverpool docks and they were huge!

Steve Pibworth

Nancy Ford with father William Davis, stud groom to Sam Hardy.

Horses

A Mr Fullick, who lived with his mother next to the hop kilns in Bones Lane, Buriton, was the man who looked after the carthorses. He'd had them all of his life and when the tractors came the horses all had to be destroyed and I think it must have upset Mr Fullick terribly. They all had names and were absolutely beautiful; we children used to ride up to the hop fields on their backs but they were so wide we had to sit the other way round because we couldn't put our little legs astride them! While the hops were drying on the drying floor, the engine would rumble all night. The noise and smell at hop-picking time was beautiful.

June Edwards

Mr Fyander

My father was stud groom to Sam Hardy, a very rich man who came up from Bath (with my father and his brother, Harry) in about 1910. He had stabling for about fourteen horses at the Causeway where I lived and he also had carriage horses, which were kept at the bottom of Dragon Street. He was Master of the Hambledon Foxhounds, which met in The Spain. The foxhounds were kept at Droxford but we had lots of other domestic dogs at The Causeway. The only thing I didn't like was when a horse died. A Mr Fyander used to come up – he had one arm and a hook on the other one – and we would block our ears up when we knew a horse was going to be shot. He used to skin them and hang them up and they would drip all day and then he would cook them in a big copper and feed the meat to the dogs. I can still remember the smell of the horse flesh cooking.

Nancy Ford

Bell Hill

I was born in 1915 and when I was four years old I lived in Bordon. I can just remember my father (James Foard) coming home from the First World War. There used to be a big timber yard where we children used to play and I can remember my father coming towards me with a stick and limping – he had

17

been wounded by a shell case. I moved to Petersfield in 1924 when I was nine years old and I lived there until I was eleven or twelve. I lived with my father and my brother, Herbert. I had an older brother and a sister but they didn't live with us; Jim worked on an estate a long way away and my sister Ida was in service. Herbert and I had to look after ourselves. Father was a carpenter on Mr Shuttleworth's estate. His housekeeper was a Mrs Adams and she had a huge sheepdog in the house. She used to put bits of meat on high shelves but the dog always found it. I lived in a very poor but pretty little cottage at the top of Bell Hill. It had a well right in front of the front door, the path was edged with golden rod and there was a little orchard at the back. Jewish people lived next door; the children were at boarding school but when they came home for their holidays I used to play with them and we got on very well, we didn't think of race in those days.

Ernest Foard

Gas lights

As I got older I was allowed out on winter evenings and two or three of us would meet by the old gas works in Hylton Road. There was an earth path by the roadside where we would mark out a ring and play marbles – the old gas lamp shining above us gave us all the light we needed. Steve Hudson was the lamplighter in those days. He had a long pole with a hook on it and he would ride round the town and put all the lights on and off. At home we had a paraffin lamp in the kitchen-cum-living room, and when we went into the front room (as a treat on a Sunday or Christmas time) Mum had a double burner oil lamp which had a green oil container with a lovely spotted glass bowl shade which we thought was wonderful. The light we used to go to bed was a candle in a candlestick – no gas, no electric – and yet we could see to read alright.

Harry Edwards

The lamplighter

The gas lamplighter used to come on a bike at dusk. He had a long pole and he would be able to push up the lever (it had a little 'flicker' on it) and that would light the street lamp. When electricity arrived everything changed.

Earnest Foard

Feather bed

I loved going to my grandparents' old cottage at No. 14 Sussex Road, Petersfield. The whole front of the house was covered with slates and there used to be a well just inside the yard door; inside it was so small, with a little windy staircase. They had the gas light outside the window and I loved sleeping in grandmother's feather bed and seeing that glow through the window; we had no streetlights in Buriton and so lights were a luxury. The inside of the cottage was lit by oil lamps and grandmother had a cabinet filled with stuffed birds as well as two real cats, two canaries in a cage and a parrot which my uncle had brought back from abroad when he was in the Navy. The cottage is still there but the slates have been taken off the front, which is a shame; you used to be able to warm your hands on them.

June Edwards

Sunday school

The Salvation Army was somewhere to go and I was a boy soldier, as they called it then. They used to sell the *War Cry* (newspaper) in the town. The Citadel was in Swan Street. I

Lucy and Harry Edwards, June Edwards' grandparents at 14 Sussex Road (Goldenball Road), c. 1920.

remember one Christmas party: I had my trousers done up with a tie and the tie broke so when I went up for my present I was holding my trousers up! I got a box of lead soldiers – if I had them now they would be worth a fortune. I used to go to the Sunday School as a young soldier but my sister was better – she had the full uniform and everything. They were very kind to us and of course the Salvation Army was very good to the soldiers in the war; I have a lot of respect for the Salvation Army.

Earnest Foard

Sharing

Mother used to send me to Sunday School and one day I got a real telling off from Canon Morley, the vicar of St Mary's, Buriton. He'd been telling all the little children that we must share everything so, when Sunday School was finished, I went out into the churchyard and saw that somebody had all these wonderful flowers on their grave and there weren't any on anybody else's, so I spent hours putting flowers on everybody's grave from this huge bunch that was there. I couldn't understand why I was told off by the vicar because he had just told us to share things!

June Edwards

Weather

The Liss and Hill Brow road sweeper in the 1950s was Bill Lintott. He was a bachelor and lived in Mint Road, Liss. Bill would be seen cutting back all the overgrown hedges in the lanes, using a 'fag hook', which was a bit like a scythe. More importantly, Bill was a font of all knowledge. He knew everything about the area and was even able to give accurate weather forecasts. He was well known and loved by the whole village.

Jennifer Robinson

Lost

The electricity boards from all over the country came to help us after the great storm of 1987. I was told that a team of five or six chaps were coming from the Irish Electricity Board so I said I would go and meet them, just behind the Petersfield station. They were supposed to arrive at about 10 a.m. but by 11 no one had heard from them. I went away and came back a couple of hours later to find they'd just arrived. I said, 'You're very welcome, it is very good of you to come, did you have a bad journey?' They said, 'No, no we had a very good journey, we just couldn't find the end of the M25!' They'd been told to come down the M1 and round the M25 and then turn off onto the A3, but they carried on and they'd been round the M25 twice! Very Irish!

Michael Mates MP

Floods

The end of Rushes Road used to flood regularly until they made an alteration to the drainage. I can remember there was a dressmaker who lived on the corner and around her sitting room was a mark where the floods used to come. The mark was a good two feet high.

Nancy de Combe

Daisy cart

I was about three when we moved to Rose Cottage, North Lane, in Buriton. All our belongings were moved by the farm cart which was pulled by the big shire-horses and one of my earliest memories was of sitting high on the top of that cart. Wonder of wonders, the new cottage had running water and electricity! We actually had a tap inside! Previously, my mother had to walk down to the tap, which was on the wall by the old hop kilns, for all our water. If it was frozen in the winter it was impossible. There was also a tap in the High Street for the farm labourers' cottages. We never had any drainage though and the toilets were in a little hut at the end of the garden. I was terrified to go down the cinder path in the dark, and when I got there I would look round for all the spiders with the torch and get out again as quick as I could. It wasn't until after the war that we got an inside toilet. Father used to dig a huge pit in the garden to empty the bucket and he said we had the best rhubarb in the village! Then we used to have what we

Two views of the floods in Petersfield.

called the Daisy Cart that came round in the night, once a week, to empty these soiled buckets into a big container; everybody used to shut their windows that night.

June Edwards

Strood not Strowd!

Stroud only became a village with a parish in 1995 and up until that time half the village was looked upon as being in the St Peter's ward, which is actually Petersfield, and the other half was in the parish of Langrish. When the motorway was put in it made a natural boundary between Petersfield and Stroud so it was thought that it would be good if Stroud was a village in its own right, with its own parish, and that is when it actually broke away from Petersfield. Langrish only became a parish in 1894 because up until that time the parish of East Meon came all the way up to approximately Ramsdean Road in Stroud. So, Langrish and Stroud haven't had their own parishes for very long – 100 years for Langrish and only eight years for Stroud.

The town of Petersfield was originally thought to be a small settlement in a field on the estate of the ancient Mapledurham Manor, which was in Buriton, two miles south of the present-day Petersfield. The settlement had a chapel that was dedicated to St Peter – hence the name Petersfield. Between Mapledurham Manor and the Manors of Langrish and East Meon was what they called the wasteland and this was known as 'the stroud' – an old term meaning marsh or wetland. Our village of Stroud lies on the common in the stroud, within the valley between the Downs and the Hangars, with the Criddle Stream running through it. People like my grandparents would always say they lived in *the* Stroud, the word 'the' was always paramount, but now you never hear it. If Stroud is the youngest of our villages, Buriton is the oldest. Lots of people

who are new to Stroud call it 'Strowd' not 'Strood', which is the correct Hampshire pronunciation; I am always tempted to correct people and have to keep biting my tongue.

Clinton Brown

Age Concern

Much to my horror, I recently realised that I have been Chairman of Age Concern since 1978; I have just gone on and on so I'm going to hand in my resignation! Age Concern has changed out of all recognition since the days when I used to go to the villages and talk to them; it was bingo and a cup of tea and the meetings only cost about 5d. It is an entirely different world now. When I took over we had thirteen small branches, right down to Rowlands Castle, but we are now down to six because we have an absolutely different

Clinton Brown, 2003.

concept of 'old age' these days. Old age used to start at fifty – you were eligible to go to our luncheon club at fifty, use our minibus and so on, but now at fifty you're still young and down at the gym! And of course, what is so lovely is that the business and marketing world is realising that we elderly do have a lot to offer society and that we often work part time, well into our seventies.

Elsa Bulmer

Petersfield to Pennsylvania

We are related to the William Penn who left Portsmouth for America and founded Pennsylvania. Three of the Penn brothers married the three Alford sisters and they all went to live on the Isle of Wight. Charlie Penn became a famous Isle of Wight horse dealer and farmer who came to the Taro Fair every year and, for some reason, no one would bid against him; as a small child in Stroud he was famous for having a wooden leg. Robert Penn was quite a dapper man but he was the black sheep of the family. He was a petty criminal and a bit of a rogue but he became the first rat catcher on the Isle of Wight and he would often make quite a bit of money. His son, Frank, said that when his father had money he would drop him off with a gypsy family and go off to Portsmouth to gamble (and everything that goes with it) and days later he would come back for him, but while he was away my aunts and uncles would get Frank and bring him to stay with the family in Stroud. The third brother was Tom who worked on various farms on the Isle of Wight and returned to Steep to work on the Soal Farm.

My grandfather was born in Sheet in 1875 and he and my grandmother, Rebekah (Knight), grew up together before marrying in 1900. The reception was held at Cook's Farm – now Malstock Farm. Their first home was Mount Pleasant Farm in Ramsdean Road,

Steep, which had originally been known as the Pest House! The house was built on the furthest reach of the parish of East Meon and when people had diseases, such as smallpox and cholera, they were put in the Pest House – in other words, the isolation hospital. There is a plaque to this effect on the front of the house but very few people notice it. My great grandmother, Rhoda Knight, lived in the cottage next door so when my grandmother got married she just moved next door into the farmhouse!

Clinton Brown

New Year

Because we three were all very close in age we had married about the same time and so, in the 1950s, there were eleven grandchildren who were all very much the same age; my sister had five children, my brother had three and I had three. My father, who was a very reserved man but with a dry sense of humour, used to celebrate New Year's Eve with a ship's bell that came from HMS *Conquest*. The naval custom is that the New Year is rung in with a double eight bells (sixteen bells) and on New Year's Eve the youngest person staying in the house would ring in the New Year on this ship's bell. It used to ring out all over Hill Brow! He would even get the poor child out of bed to ring it; it was quite a ritual. On New Year's Day in 1960, my father, in his rather dry humorous way said, 'Well, with eleven grandchildren in ten years, it has certainly been the fertile fifties: I do hope it is followed by the sterile sixties!'

Caroline Kennedy (née Bickford-Smith)

Jersey cream

I was lucky enough to be brought up on a smallholding; we had three Jersey cows, a

Mount Pleasant Farm, known around 1700 as the Pest House – home for incurable diseases, such as the plague and smallpox.

A sign on the wall of Mount Pleasant Farm, Ramsdean Road, Stroud. The Pest House for Incurables was in the parish of East Meon, which included Stroud.

The wedding of Rebekah and George Penn, on 15 September 1900. This photograph shows three generations of a Stroud family: Knight, Penn and Windybank.

Guernsey, half-a-dozen sheep, pigs and about fifty or sixty chickens and ducks – a whole menagerie. My father used to go out first thing in the morning before he went to work, milk the cow and bring the milk in a stainless-steel bucket to the back room, where my mother would be waiting with china bowls with muslin cloths over the top. Jersey cows had wonderful cream on their milk so mother would skim it off first. Up until we lost my father the only bottled milk I ever had was at school. Mother made her own butter but my grandmother used to make 200 pounds of butter a week which she would take into the Petersfield market to be sold. We've still got the butter churns at home. Sadly, you don't see the Jersey herds around here any more. My father died when I was only eight years old and I think my childhood probably helped me to come to terms with that. That is one of the reasons I have chickens, rabbits and guinea pigs for my children now.

Clinton Brown

Reeves removals

My father had a farm in East Meon called Lower Farm, which he rented from Lady Peel from 1912. He would move over there on 5 April every year and return on 5 October; in the meantime Hardy House in The Spain would be decorated. Reeves Removals would move his paintings and favourite pieces of furniture by horse and cart, and after the First World War they used army surplus vans. One day the van broke down and they didn't know how to fix it. Father was so horrified to find his possessions sitting on the Winchester Road that he insisted they got the cart and horses out; thereafter, Reeves used only horse-drawn vehicles to move the Hardys to East Meon! When asked why he took paintings to the farm father always said, 'If the King can move

his things from Balmoral to Sandringham, why shouldn't I move mine from Petersfield to East Meon?'

Charles Hardy

Living over the shop

We lived behind and above the hairdressing shop and it was a tough life for a child; we always had staff walking in and out of the house and I grew up having adults around me all the time. It was almost impossible to invite friends home. I was always in the shop with my father. In those days we had cubicles and I sat on a small chair in the cubicle to watch him. Hairdressing was almost inbred in me, even when I was ill in bed my father would bring me a block with a wig and he would say, 'There you are, you can learn pin curls'. I learnt how to hold a comb the correct way and I would comb all the fur on my teddy – I cut my poor teddy's hair and made him quite bald! I didn't know any other life, mine was just hairdressing.

Margaret Maybray (née Lee)

18/19 The Square

Ours is a straight building that goes down towards St Peter's Road and the property alongside us was once used by the coach builders, Cox & Son; in one part there is a pit where they used to work under the coaches. We took that under our wing in the 1920s and we purchased our property from Magdalen College, Cambridge, at the same time. It was great fun when we had the building restored! It is a grade II listed building and it hadn't been touched for over 100 years. In the early '90s the heritage side of the district council told us we had to do something about it, or they would do it for us and charge us a lot of money. We got help and grants from the

Rowland Son & Vincent, 18/19 The Square. (Copyright Rowland Son & Vincent)

Hampshire County Council and English Heritage and the district council were very involved. Every time we moved something we found something else! The front of the building was bowed out and we found that it was only the weight of the tiles that was keeping the roof on – it was an absolute nightmare. We found a staircase in the basement which is either Elizabethan or Tudor and only about six steps high; we also found a bread oven in the basement and a very pretty little Victorian fireplace up in the roof. We now know that the foundations of the building are 1482 and probably started life as a private house. We reckon it cost the price of a small terrace of houses to restore but we managed – with a lot of help. My father used to say that the major work on the shop would happen long after he'd gone – we began about four years after he died!

Mary Vincent

2 Schooldays

Petersfield schools

The school that has shown the most staggering improvement is the Petersfield School and that is largely due to a superb head teacher, Katherine Bell, who retired two years ago. She brought it up by its bootstraps. Petersfield has got three thoroughly good secondary schools – two of them happen to be independent and one state, all doing music together and playing sport against each other. All the feeder schools are also good; you can't get into the Sheet Primary School because it is so popular. I'm very happy that we got them an extra building; that is the satisfying bit of my job, when you can get a primary school a new building simply by going and knocking on the doors of the powers-that-be and saying, 'Oi!'.

Michael Mates MP

Girls against boys

I was at Petersfield School when boys and girls were separated and the girls had a lovely mistress, Miss Sutherland, who taught us embroidery and how to be ladylike and to like nice things. We were so sad when they changed the school to mixed and we had to go up and be with the boys – the girls hated it! We all ganged up against the boys. There were always empty seats because three girls would crowd in the seats made for two so that we didn't have to be bothered with the boys.

Nevertheless, we were very well taught. We used to skip with skipping ropes and I remember when they tarred the road and all the sand was thrown on top of the tar. We used to run home and up to the station because the taxi, which was a horse and cart, used to be there and we used to sit on the back of the cart and have a ride. The other boys and girls walked, so we always got there first and they used to shout out 'Whip behind mister!' Mr Gates and Mr Bennets were very musical and we had lots of singing. I belonged to the Brownies at that time and we went to the Petersfield Musical Festival to sing. Sir Adrian Boult and Sir Malcolm Sargent sometimes conducted.

Phyllis Gilburd

Illness

I was born at No. 75 Rushes Road, Petersfield, in 1921, and then when I was two-and-a-half, we moved to a cottage in St Peter's Road, near the school where I was educated. I absolutely hated school, from the time I started to the time I left. The day I left I wouldn't go into school because I didn't want to shake hands with all the teachers! We lived too close to the school, I suppose; I was so close that I went home for all my meals. I cried every day when I first started. I wouldn't eat, so, to get me better, Mummy (Kate Tipper) had to buy steak, scrape it between bread and butter and put sugar on it. To make things worse, shortly

Petersfield Girls School. Phyllis Gilburd (née Danby) is pictured middle row, third from left.

after starting school, I was home for a year with double pneumonia and pleurisy; they didn't take you away in those days so my mother nursed me night and day, with two doctors coming all the time. No traffic was allowed to go by the cottage, no church bells rang and they put straw on the ground outside our house. I was home a year so I lost out on making friends. I never took a lot of interest and I was eventually put in what they called the 'adjustment class', more or less a dunces class – my brother-in-law was in there with me and he died with lots of money, but I'm no better off! My husband, Harry, was a twin and we all went to school together. Rene (Irene Chapman) was my teacher when I was in the seniors and then my cousin married Rene so we are a little bit related. Seniors wasn't any better but in those days we had open fires to heat the school and that was nice.

Nancy de Combe

Afternoons off!

I went to the Petersfield School in St Peter's Road and there I stayed until I was ten when I won a scholarship to the Petersfield School for girls (in the old Dolphin Hotel). I was there very soon after it opened and I stayed for seven years – I enjoyed my schooldays very much. It was a very old building with smelly cellars – we weren't supposed to go down there but we did. At the back of the Dolphin there was one large covered yard where the horses used to go when it was a coaching inn. There was also a very big shed that had been the horses' stables but in my day it was used as a bicycle shed. I had curvature of the spine during my school days so every afternoon, when fine, I used to go into the headmistress' small garden and there I used to lie on a form, supported by two chairs. When it was wet I would lie on the Headmistress' chaise longue in her sitting room, so I had no afternoon schooling at all.

Irene Chapman

Growing vegetables

At first I went to a private school at the bottom of Ramshill which was run by a Mrs Bennett. Then they sent me to Sheet until I was eleven and afterwards I went to the Petersfield Secondary School in St Peter's Road until I was fourteen. I had a very basic education but it was a happy time. Everybody was given garden plots in those days and we grew vegetables. At the end of term all the products were sold on parents' day. One classroom was stepped up in levels with no balcony railings – we could have fallen off, but we didn't.

John Freeman

A dab of sherbert

I went to the little Petersfield School when a Mr Gates was the headmaster and I believe that the patron of the school was Nurse Edith Cavell. The school was lovely and I did very well there. We had a tuck shop (I think it was on the way down to The Spain) where they used to do a packet of popcorn for a ha'penny and a little dab of sherbet shaped like a triangle, also for a ha'penny. I left school three or four weeks before my fourteenth birthday; in those days, schools used to break up early to enable the children to work on the estates, getting the hay in and things. I went to work the very next Monday and straight away I paid ninepence a week National Health Insurance. My weekly wage was nine shillings and eventually I was working fifty or sixty hours a week for that.

Earnest Foard

Air Cadets

When we were eleven we all went into the Petersfield Secondary Modern, which is where the infants' school is now, in St Peter's Road. I didn't like senior school very much, but who likes school when they are teenagers? When we were fourteen, someone came round to tell us we ought to join the Air Cadets so we went to the Chapel Hall in Petersfield and saw a Mrs Clutterbuck to be fitted out with a uniform. That was OK until we came to the shoes, and not for the life of me would I join up if I had to wear these awful black lace-up shoes – so that was the end of my career in the Air Cadets!

June Edwards

Lessons in the garden

I went to Miss William's school at Winton House. It had a lot of land, including a field (now the central car park) with a big walnut tree in the middle. We played rounders and other games down there and in the summer we often did our lessons in the garden. We would walk along the stream, through where Burgess Mead is now, to where Mr George Bailey grew vegetables in greenhouses for his shop. We had Thursday afternoons off in those days and we had a Brownie group in the school, run by Miss Leigh (after the war I knew her as Mrs Balance).

When we were ten we moved across to the Petersfield High School, in the old Dolphin Hotel, and in 1919 the county made it the Petersfield Girls County High School. Miss Emma Lowde was the headmistress, and I had great respect for her – she had a very good sense of humour. We had a tennis court and a hard netball court on the area that is now a car park. Between the school building and St Peter's Road there was only one house and the electricity offices. Miss Lowde would try to

*Petersfield Infants,
c. 1910. Harry Edwards
is in the back row, in a
sailor suit.*

*Petersfield Boys School,
1912. Harry Edwards is
second on the right, second
row from back.*

*Pictured from left to right,
in front, are: Joyce Blake,
Audrey Dabbs, Miss
Clutterbuck and Diana
Heighes. Behind them are
Irene Brown and Gillian
Holt (both obscured), and
June Edwards.*

Petersfield School, c. 1920. Mabel Edwards (Harry's sister) is second on the left, second row down.

interest us in things that were happening locally and one day there was a discussion about the Petersfield bypass – in 1936! She said that somehow she didn't think the thing would materialise until we second-form girls were grandmothers, and it was an absolutely true prophecy! It was 1993 when the Petersfield bypass actually opened and by that time I had nine of my eleven grandchildren!

I wanted to be a meteorologist but I couldn't do physics at the Petersfield School, so I moved over to the Portsmouth High School (which had been evacuated to Adhurst St Mary during the war) and did my High Certification, which included physics and maths. When I left school I had been glad to get away from Petersfield but when we came back in 1950 I joined the staff of the Petersfield High School and taught until Alistair was born in 1952.

Mary Ray

Lunchtime

I first went to school in what was the Commercial Hotel in The Square. It was a little private school and there were only about five of us with one teacher. I then went to Miss Richardson's school in Sandringham Road, up towards what used to be the Itside Rubber Factory. I hated school. We used to have to play the piano in front of everybody. After that I went to the Petersfield Girls School. Miss Syme was our teacher, Mr Gates was the headmaster – he lived in the playground of the junior school; Mr Hammond taught geography, and I think he had been to Africa. Ever since then I have been very interested in Africa. Mr Bennett was the music teacher; the cookery teacher was Miss Bebb and she taught us in a little building which is down the path where the museum is now. Mother used to send my lunch down with one of the stable boys and when it rained we were allowed to go there and have our lunch. I left school when I was fourteen.

Nancy Ford

Churcher's college

The tragedy for Petersfield occured when Churcher's College went independent, which is something I never quite understood about the Socialist government. It was a thoroughly good voluntary aided school, but then the Labour government took away their grant so they had to go private, which meant that the bright children of poor parents in Petersfield didn't have a school. Then we put in the assisted places scheme so that the poor children could get back there again (if they were bright enough). Now this Labour government has taken that away. It is ridiculous.

Michael Mates MP

Prep school

I went to Churcher's preparatory school in Heath Harrison House, which is within the school grounds and where the headmaster lives now. The headmaster was Mr Jack Legrice. He used to play football with us and he was the first man that I can remember that used to juggle with a football, keeping the ball up like the modern footballers. I used to do a terrific lot of cross–country running at school as well as rugger and cricket, and I played soccer for Petersfield and Sheet. Before we started in the morning, Mr Legrice would take us for a walk down Kingsfernden Lane and we'd look at all the plants and weeds and so on, it was excellent. The prep school was quite small, just four classes and about fifty boys. I moved up to the college where my brother, John David, was already a pupil. He

Old boys of Churchers College (sons of W.J. Chapman).

later went into the Royal Engineers and was terribly wounded in Normandy.

Steve Pibworth

Baa!!

George Schofield MBE was the headmaster of Churcher's College when I was there. He was an inspired headmaster: although a scientist, he used to encourage performances of Shakespeare in the Easter term and Gilbert and Sullivan every other year. The first one was *HMS Pinafore* in about 1949 and the second, in 1951, was *Pirates of Penzance*. That got me interested in the stage. Tim Warden Lane and his wife Brenda were good musicians and very good at coaching. Tim's subject was history and he had a good sense of humour; you'd always know where his class was because they'd all be laughing. He had a Morris 8 with the registration of BAA109

Above left: *The Curiosity Shop, The Square c. 1944. On the left is Marjorie Bullough, and on the right, Margaret Lee (now Maybrey). This photograph was taken by prize-winning amateur photographer Mr Milner, pharmacist with Boots the chemist.*

Above right: *Margaret Maybrey outside the same window in 2003.*

and you would hear the whole class erupt with 'Baa!' Of course he was also known as Larry! Gus Kershaw taught English and produced the Shakespeare examination play. We knew the play off by heart and consequently there was nothing we couldn't quote, although we might not have known what we were saying!

Ken Hick

Buriton school

I was a bit of a loner because I had no brothers or sisters. I didn't really like other children; I preferred animals. I would go off to the fields for ages on my own – couldn't do it these days. I didn't mind school but I hated playtime – all those children rushing around making a lot of noise. Miss Pleasant, the head teacher of Buriton School, would find me hiding in a corner of the playground so she used to take me in and sit me on her knee and she'd read me a story. I ran away once, which caused chaos; I ended up in some little cottage in Toads Alley. A lady had seen me wandering along and had taken me in. She gave me a chocolate biscuit and then sent for my father. I was missing for a whole day. Nobody worried the way they would these days because people were kind and everybody knew everybody else. Later on I got to know that boys were fun to be with because they climbed trees and did the things I liked to do.

I once got into trouble. I was going to Sunday school in a beautiful red coat my mother had made me and the boys from North Lane dared me to climb this tree; I heard the horrible noise of ripping and when I got down there was a tear right down the back of the coat.

June Edwards

Langrish school

Like all my family I went to the Langrish School, and my two children, Joshua and Jasmine, go there now. That is another anomaly that people can't work out. They think that Langrish School should be in Langrish, but it's not, it's in Stroud. The reason is that Langrish School outgrew itself in 1914 and they built the new school in Stroud but still kept the name, so that's why it's called Langrish School.

Clinton Brown

Steep school

I went to Steep school and my mother used to feed my friends in the kitchen. We had an old black-leaded kitchen range and she would give us cheese on toast and we would play table tennis in the (Harrow) bar. Of course, we didn't have television or radio; somebody in Steep Marsh was the first to have a radio and so to listen to Dick Barton we all had to go through Kettlebrook, which was a very dark area.

Ellen McCutcheon

Longmoor garrison school

I went to Longmoor Garrison School and a couple of soldiers would come down and arrange sports for us. We had a pond where we used to go swimming and they organised swimming competitions. They also put up some parallel bars out in the wood and we did running and a bit of boxing. We went to Hayling Island with the Scouts in 1919. Miss Papillion, from Liss, ran the troop. Two soldiers came down to help for the week, a Sergeant Judd and a Corporal Bowling. While we were there we met up with a troop of Scouts from London and so the soldiers arranged sports competitions for us all. We didn't do very well!

Norman Gilburd

Bedales

I was a teacher at Bedales for over twenty years, and spent time as a housemistress before becoming deputy head and then head. It is a unique and very special environment, and its countryside setting contributes strongly to its atmosphere and ethos.

Bedales has been in Steep for over a century now, having moved to its present site in the winter of 1900, to what was then a farm with nearly 200 acres of land. Although some of the existing eighteenth and nineteenth-century houses were incorporated into the footprint and daily life of the school, many of the more important buildings date from the period from 1900 to 1920. These include some significant Arts and Crafts structures such as the Lupton Hall (1911) and the renowned Memorial Library designed by Edward Barnsley (1920). There are also some beautiful newer buildings, my favourite being the stunning Olivier Theatre.

It is still a remarkable school today. Although many of the more striking features – coeducation being an obvious example – have been taken up widely by others, there are still many aspects that make it an unusual place. When John Badley founded the school in 1893, at the height of the Victorian era, he

Olivier Theatre, Bedales School.

wanted an environment where many of the normal rules, regulations and constraints of the established boarding schools of the age could be safely set aside; where children would be free to grow into the characters they were destined to be, without forcing them into a mould. The curriculum was – and still is – unusually broad, attempting to educate Head, Heart and Hand; emphasis was placed on the Arts, but not at the expense of other areas; children were encouraged to spend time working outside, on the land, as well as in the classroom. Relationships were felt to be at the very heart of what the school stood for, which remains a priority today with first names used by everyone, from the youngest child to the Head.

It is still recognisably the same school, although an extensive building programme is fast changing the visual landscape and the requirements of modern education have inevitably necessitated additions and changes

to the curriculum over the decades. But the liberal, child-centred ethos remains, and there is an exceptional 'buzz' about the place which people don't find elsewhere. I certainly loved it.

There are so many stories and anecdotes – almost too many to remember and some of them probably best forgotten! I do remember one winter's afternoon when English master John Batstone passed me walking away from the Quad, having just experienced what he called 'the best and worst' of Bedales life. On his way to teach a lesson, he had paused momentarily at the edge of the Quad while a young girl practised Elgar's cello concerto in preparation for a concert. The light was fading, the music was sublime, and the girl was utterly engrossed: it was one of those wonderful, inspiring moments that lift one above the trials and tribulations of the day. As he listened, he laid his hand down on the piano nearby, only to feel an ominous squelch

First Sheet Brownie pack, c. 1954. From left to right, back row: Patsy Stevens, -?-, Thelma Wickins, Pat Carey, Doreen Hoare, Celia ?, Jill Armstrong, -?-, Diana Lloyd, -?-. Front row: Christine Reeves, Marion Johnson, Ben Foster (vicar), Mrs Pam Dowler (Brown Owl), the Girl Guide District Commissioner, -?-, Jenneth Gilburd.

under his fingers. He looked down to find a half-eaten, discarded jam sandwich, probably left there by the girl herself! It occurred to him that this summed up the very worst and very best of Bedales life.

Alison Willcocks

Thoroughly good

Bedales School is a thoroughly good part of Petersfield life. They do lots of good things outside the school. All the children go out to the handicapped schools on a regular basis to play with the kids; my daughter, Arabella, goes to Meadowlands and plays music with them. And, of course, Bedales has got that lovely theatre which is open to the public.

Michael Mates MP

3 Working Life

First ladies' hairdressers

My grandfather, Henry ('Harry') Lee was born in the East End of London but in the 1890s he came to Petersfield and joined old Mr John Freeman in his barber shop in Chapel Street. In 1898 he decided to branch out on his own and opened Lee's Hairdressers (for men and children) in Station Road. It had the barber's red and white pole outside, and a sign advertising, 'Gents Barbers and Shaving – clean water used for every shave'. In 1911 he moved to 6 High Street but in 1918 he moved to the much larger shop at No. 13 The Square where he was able to offer both ladies' and gentlemen's hairdressing. My father William (Bill) Lee then joined him and the shop was renamed H. Lee & Son. Sadly, No. 13 was eventually pulled down to make way for the construction of what is now Rams Walk. Our house would have been at the High Street entrance of Rams Walk and the Walk was actually our garden with the river at the bottom.

Bill Lee was the eldest son of nine children and over the years Edith, Jack and Fred joined the business. Jack added a new dimension by repairing umbrellas and sunshades (Grandma recovered them) and selling walking sticks. Jim, Doris and Eric were not hairdressers but Ethel became a hairdresser and worked in Reading (the two other children died in infancy). After my grandfather died in 1930 it became Lee Brothers. Mr Edmund Fleetwood worked in the shop as a barber from 1928 until 1984.

Father was one of the first people in the south of England ever do a Vapour Marcel perm; that must have been in the late 1920s or early '30s. Then the MacDonald perm came in and that was done right up until the 1950s. The MacDonald perm was a spiral wave: you wound the hair onto rods from the roots to the end (as opposed to working from the ends to the roots) with gauzes and strings with little buckets on the end; a chemical was put into the top of the machine and in the buckets. You had rubbers to stop the heat from burning the client; we had to be careful – you could easily get burnt – but we rarely did. The MacDonald perm never damaged the hair – it was very mild. At the end of the perm you had to wind all the strings up and clean the machine and prepare it for the next client – that was one of my jobs when I was quite small. The perm would take several hours so we could only do one perm at a time and never more than two a day. Later, the steamless perms came in and then the MacDonald Cool Wave Machine was brought out; this entailed winding the hair with gentle heat. In the early 1950s we charged £2 10s and people expected their perms to last a year – they wouldn't cut their hair until the next perm. The Marcel Waving was done with hot curling irons heated on gas burners, but that was only temporary, a bit like today's blow-dry, and that would cost about 2s.

Father was in his element in the 1920s because he was very good at blow-drying. He didn't use a brush; he did it with combs.

Clockwise from top left:

Harry Lee, Station Road in the 1900s.

Harry Lee, 13 The Square, c. 1920.

Judy the cat, in the garden of Lee Bros., 13 The Square (now Rams Walk!), during the early 1950s.

He had combs of about four inches long and about one-and-a-half inches deep and he would push them into each wave and direct the hot air down to make the hair bend. He used to blow-wave my hair as a child – it is certainly not a modern method. We had hair dryers with long tubes fixed to a round thing on the wall which we could walk around with, but later we had the ones with sort of fingers – round tubes with holes – these were on stands and quite modern! The hood styles used today came in during the late 1940s.

My favourite era of hair was the natural-looking styles in about 1952 when rollers first came in; they were metal in those days and we didn't use them all over, only in places. When my brother and I said, 'Come on Dad, get some of these rollers, they're new' he said, 'They're not new, we had them in the 1930s but they were made of crêpe hair and were called 'Biggledeys'. Crêpe hair is still used in wigs for the theatre.

Margaret Maybrey

Clockwise from top left:

A carnival float in the 1930s, with the MacDonald perming machine. From left to right: Fred, Bill, Edith and Jack Lee in MacDonald tartan.

Bill Lee outside No. 13 The Square. Next door were Edward Privett, outfitters, where clothes were made on the premises until the late 1950s.

Harry and Elizabeth Lee, c. 1910, with Ethel, Bill, Doris, Jack (on Elizabeth's knee) and Jim (on the floor).

First gentlemen's hairdressers

My grandfather, John William Freeman, was born in 1853. He came from Kent to Petersfield in 1876 and started the first gentlemen's hairdressing business in Petersfield at No. 13, Chapel Street. Initially, he ran a combined toy and hairdressing business. My father, William Moon Freeman, was an assistant to him until he was called up for the First World War. When he came out of the army in 1919 he bought the business off his father and in 1923 he moved it to 17 Chapel Street and began offering a limited ladies hairdressing service in an upstairs room, but we didn't continue with that for long. When my grandfather retired, father took on Mr Harold White as his assistant. In 1930 he bought 11a Chapel Street, which was just the other side of where grandfather had started all those years ago. He made that property into two shops, one for the hairdressing and the other he let to Mr and Mrs Bannister, the jewellers. That building had originally been a butcher's shop and slaughterhouse with a plaster bull's head on the wall. There was a copper pan where they used to boil pigs to get the hairs off and a manger for the horse. When I retired, the shop was redeveloped and became Kimber's shoe shop and the bull's head was moved out the back; it's still there now but most people don't notice it.

I came into the family business in 1935 when I was fourteen years old. I didn't like shaving when I first started. Old men used to come in and have a shave once a week but they didn't shave in-between time, so you can imagine what that was like! An American came in once for a haircut and he said 'Could you trim my back?' I said, 'I've already trimmed your neck', but he said 'No, I said my back'. So he took his shirt off and he wanted me to shave his back! He said 'I don't like going skiing with hair on my back'. Of course when he left, everyone shrieked with laughter!

After my father died in 1968, I formed a partnership with Richard Baker because I wanted to introduce a younger element to the business. We modernised the shop and put in hydraulic chairs and so on. I used to like dressing the windows and Richard would clean them! When we were at 17 Chapel Street the shop windows were filled with gifts, which the customers could exchange for coupons from Kensitas Cigarette packets. When the cigarette company changed the selection of gifts, we were allowed to keep the ones in the window. When I retired in 1985 I sold that property and Mr Baker carried on in

Freeman's hairdressers, 17 Chapel Street, c. 1923.

John William Freeman with his father William Moon Freeman in the 1950s.

other premises in Chapel Street; he retired quite recently. Our partnership lasted for sixteen years and we never had a cross word.

John Freeman

Nursing

When I was eighteen I started work as a probationary nurse at the Petersfield Cottage Hospital, near the Forge; I signed on for two years and stayed three. Unfortunately I didn't qualify as a nurse because I married in 1940, when I was twenty-one, and when my husband George was medically discharged from the army I had to look after him. I would hate anybody to think I was qualified but I knew enough about nursing to work for all the older doctors. It was all for about a guinea a time but, even though I went out to work to make ends meet, if I thought people couldn't pay me I didn't worry.

It was an excellent hospital and a nice looking building – we even had a tennis court. The men's ward was downstairs and the ladies' upstairs. I stood on the corner and wept when they pulled it down. They don't even operate in the new hospital, do they? We had the very best surgeons: Lord Horder, the Queen's physician who lived in Steep, Admiral Wakely, Mr Stanley Hillman, Mr Ridout – one of the very old type of ear, nose and throat specialists, and Mr Foley, the gynaecologist. We operated practically every day.

We had a very good theatre nurse, Sister Green, and then there was Sister Merryfield who would put any sergeant major to shame, all starch and very fierce! There was no sitting on the beds in those days; we had dresses down to our ankles, with headdresses. It was in the days when nurses lived in so we had a dining room; Matron Bates sat one end of the table and the sisters at the other and, as a probationary, you wouldn't dare say if you didn't like anything because you had to eat it!

June Walker, 2003.

Often, when I was standing at the window cleaning the sink, this gentleman used to go by on a bike and wave to me. One day I went down to see the new patients coming in and this young man said, 'You wouldn't happen to be the nurse I've been waving to, would you?' It was George – he had come in to have his appendix out – that's how we met. George was an electrician and he worked for the Southern Electricity Board for well over forty years. He retired at sixty-five but died the next year. It was a very happy year though, as we went to Canada to see our daughter.

June Walker

Library

The Petersfield Library moved around the town before arriving in this lovely new building in June 1981. In the 1920s it was above a butcher's shop in the High Street

The Petersfield Library at Winton House, c. 1945.

before moving to the Working Men's Club. In 1937 it relocated to the newly-built Town Hall but in September 1939 the ARP took the room over and the library retreated to the Working Men's Club. In 1945 it moved to Winton House and in 1978 I joined the team.

We occupied the ground floor of Winton House with the YWCA on the top two floors. We operated from a number of very small rooms. We had to do all our administrative work in an old scullery; the reference library was about 8ft square; the children's library was a little room in the back; the lending library was in two different rooms with a corridor in between and the office was round the side, which is now the alleyway that goes up to the Folly Market. The mobile library used to have to park outside in the street in order to load up the stock. We didn't have space for many books but we were still quite busy and in those days we had to find room for the card catalogue, all of which is now on computer.

The warden of the YWCA used to boil cabbage and the smell would permeate the library. The building was constantly falling apart and when they were doing some building work upstairs, a 3ft-long crowbar fell through the ceiling and cut through a carpet, making a hole in the floor. It landed just behind Mrs Francis Mullins, one of the staff. She was hit by rubble and pieces of plaster but she wasn't hurt, just shaken. One day we looked out the window and there were several rats gambolling in the garden! We were glad to move over to the new building because the facilities were obviously much better, but we all felt we had left something behind: there was a very friendly atmosphere in Winton House and we had a close relationship with the public because of being so squashed together.

When you are dealing with the public every day it is different. Once we found a pair of false teeth in a book and another time

Inside the Petersfield Library at Winton House.

someone left her late husband in an urn on the library counter. She went away and came back later in the day looking for him! 'Have you seen my husband?' she said. We didn't ask for a description!

Des Farnham

Gammon & Smith

I was born in Bristol to Ridley Guy and Maud Pearson and came to Petersfield as a three-month-old baby; I turned up in my father's life the same week that he bought Gammon & Smith, which was a Petersfield builders' merchant. It had been a partnership of Eric Gammon and E.R. Smith. Eric Gammon was a builder as well as a merchant but in the 1920s companies didn't want to trade with a builder on merchants' terms so, in order to keep all the builders' merchants happy, Mr Gammon and Mr Smith decided they had better split up. Gammon carried on with the building company, under the name of E. Canterbury, and Smith went to Haslemere and became what my father called a 'brass plater': that is they didn't keep stock but acted as a sort of agency. Father kept the name of Gammon & Smith but would have changed it had he realised the complications of trading with companies – it took a while to persuade the manufacturers who supplied him that he was not in any way connected with a building firm. It remained as Gammon & Smith until 1994 when it was sold to Sharpe & Fisher (now Travis Perkins).

My father died in the April of 1950, just as Alan and I were going to get married in the August. We hadn't signed anything but we had almost bought a house in Epsom and I had found a teaching job there. Alan changed all his plans and decided to come back to Petersfield to run the company and we gradually expanded. I got involved and eventually became the scientist who dealt with the ready-mixed concrete. Alan died in 1992

Mary Ray, 2003.

and, although our two boys were in the business, it wasn't a good time for builders' merchants so we sold it.

Mary Ray

ITSIDE

You had plenty of jobs to choose from in 1953 and I chose ITSIDE, the rubber company at the top of Sandringham Road; I worked there for thirty-three years until it closed in 1986. After leaving school at sixteen I started working as a laboratory assistant on the testing side; I did my national service in 1956 and then when I came out I worked in the laboratory for another year before going into production as the supervisor. I became Production Manager and ended up, in the last two years of the company, as the Works Manager.

ITS, as it was first known, were the initials of the three Canadian developers of the concave/convex heel; their names were Ingwer, Tufford and Smith, and the company was formed specifically to market this new invention, the principle of which was that instead of nailing a flat heel onto a shoe, a concave/convex heel is better because it puts pressure on the sides as you push the centre, so making it tighter at the edge.

The three inventors sold the rights to the Levy family in 1919 and it set up a company in Petersfield, specifically to make these rubber heels. They changed the name to ITSIDE. They also made a resin rubber sheet that felt and looked a little like leather, in colour and texture, so the name evolved from the two products – 'ITS' and (H)IDE.

In the early 1960s, Sir Charles Colston got a golden handshake from Hoover, bought Rolls Razor (John Bloom's empire), started the Colston dishwasher, bought ITSIDE and eventually put his son, Michael, in charge. As they concentrated more on engineering rubber they reverted to the name of ITS Rubber.

The Levy family was Jewish. Arnold Levy was the Managing Director and his sons Moss, Ben and Sam were all directors of the company. One of them lived in Elsa Bulmer's house, which was used as their synagogue. The Levy's were very aloof. They would say 'hello' as they walked around the factory but they would never take their coats off and rub shoulders with the lads. Sir Charles Colston, on the other hand, was very pleasant; he would stop and talk. There would be an annual company dinner in the Town Hall and the whole factory workforce would be invited. When Michael Colston took over, Sir Charles brought him along to a dinner and introduced him as the young Mr Michael. Every year we'd get a bonus at Christmas but when things started going bad the bonus stopped without any warning, which was a bone of contention because people used to rely on it to buy Christmas presents. However, it was because of the downturn in trade so we couldn't really blame anybody for it.

There were 350 employees – it was the biggest employer in Petersfield. In the early days everything was very easy but from 1963 onwards it became a union company – the Transport and General Worker's Union – and we were under pressure all the time. The company was going through a bad time too because the footwear side was declining. They'd gone on to design a cleated commando sole and heel for the British Army but the patent for that came off around 1960 and other companies, like Bibiam and Phillips, also started to produce cleated soles. This took a lot of ITSIDE's market so, although they continued with the footwear right the way through to the finish, Colston started to move towards engineering rubber and got involved with Ford, British Leyland and Hoover. Sadly, the drop in the workforce continued and towards the end they made people redundant every summer – forty or fifty at a time, with the minimum of redundancy payouts.

Bill Lowe, 2003.

ITS was very much a part of Petersfield. Everyone would hear the hooter, which blew at eight a.m. in the morning. You had to be there three minutes after the hooter had blown, and it blew again before and after the lunch hour and at the end of the working day. We had to clock on and off; if you were late you'd get your friend to clock you on, but when you were management you had to sack people if you caught them doing what you had been doing yourself!

When I was first at ITSIDE we ate well as there was a very good canteen and they used to cook the food on the premises. As things deteriorated though the canteen was one of the first things to go. We had a social club that put on dances and we had ITSIDE cricket, darts, table tennis and football teams.

It wasn't a very good place to work; in fact it was quite horrific and a bit Dickensian. You

ITSIDE football team – Bill Lowe is wearing a sweater.

would walk into the press shop, about 100 yards long, the sun would be shining through the roof and there would be fumes everywhere. It was a rambling factory on 5½ acres and the buildings were very old. One of my jobs was employing people and I would start seven new on Monday and lose seven by Friday. The company paid what they had to, but if they'd paid more it would have been easier to keep the workforce.

We had one department called 'the black house' – an enormous department that used to mix the rubber and was always full of black dust (the main part of rubber is soot that is blended into the rubber to give it strength); it was a filthy place to work, quite disgusting. As the manager, I had to go in there but I stayed as little as possible. Strangely, that was the only place we had a steady labour force – you almost had the impression that the lads worked there because they disliked each other and they didn't want to leave in case it gave somebody else pleasure!

At first a lot of the moulding of the heels was done by women, they were physically strong with strong characters – they had to be because these moulds were 26 x 26 inches and weighed 2cwt. It was a hot job and you can imagine what it was like in the summer with a press shop full of equipment working at temperatures of 160°C, heavy work, fumes – a veritable sweatshop.

After asbestos, the rubber industry was the biggest cancer risk in industry. I had to go for a urine test every six months because lots of people in the rubber industry suffered from bladder cancer. In the early days people didn't understand what was causing it; people died but they never thought to claim compensation. We didn't have masks, just gloves to stop your hands burning. It was difficult to give people protective gear because it inhibited the way they worked; even if it was supplied it wasn't worn. We had Health Inspectors but they were more concerned with the physical side of it – whether you could trip and fall or catch your hand in the machines. The chemical side of it was not to the forefront as it is now.

Michael Colston sold the factory to a David Evans for £1, but Mr Evans also bought the debts, which were quite substantial. Mr Colston, on the other hand, sold the land for £1¼ million. David Evans proceeded to strip the company: he sold the footwear to a company called Dinky of Bristol; we used to make dog toys and he sold that to someone else. He'd bought a company at Corsham called Westbourne Engineering and he amalgamated that with ITSIDE but it eventually fell through, so ITSIDE is no longer a company.

When ITS Rubber closed I moved to a little company called Butser Rubber in Liss. It was started by Derek Winterbottom, an ex director of ITS. Derek and his wife are both dead now and his daughter and son-in-law, Nicky and Nigel Easton, run the firm. Safety and conditions are greatly improved. Up until last year I was still working in the industry and every three years I had to get a team in to monitor the air and the fumes and we had regular visits from the Health and Safety inspectors.

Bill Lowe

Petersfield bookshop

I always wanted to work in the book trade but my father was dead against it. I was too young to serve in the Second World War but I did my National Service in the Royal Navy in the late 1940s and when I was demobbed in 1956 I saw an advertisement for a bookshop manager in Petersfield. I applied and got the job, at six guineas a week. The shop was at 1 The Square (which is now the Donkey Cart)

The Petersfield bookshop, Chapel Street.

Frank and Ann Westwood, proprietors of the Petersfield bookshop, 2003.

and had been started by Flora Twort and Dr Harry Roberts, but in 1956 it was owned by a Mrs Field. When she decided to sell up she gave me the option of buying the stock; I had to sell off as much as I could, cheaply, and then I could buy what was left.

In 1959 I moved the shop to these premises in Chapel Street. They were originally stables and the Fuller's Bakery bread store, so they were full of horse collars and breadcrumbs. Later I bought the adjoining abattoir and the tobacco warehouse but I missed being close to the old market. We once had a pig in the shop which had escaped from the market! When we moved here we decided to have a go at picture framing. My assistant and I used to do it to start with and then we took someone on as a picture framer. Flora Twort framed most of her own paintings but she would come in here and straighten up all the paintings on our walls.

As we were already doing new books I kept them on, but I specialised in antique books.

We used to do a series of antique fairs but now we have narrowed it down to a couple of book fairs in London. I have found a few good books over the years. I had a nice set of Redout's *Roses*, which cost about £7,000 and is now worth about £60,000, and we once bought 5,000 books from the Howard family in Carlisle.

We do a little bit of business with the Royal family. Windsor Castle was having a job with their suppliers and my eldest son, David, who is a partner in the shop but who also works as a conservator at the Royal Library, said that we might be able to help. You have to have given good service for at least four years and you can then apply for a Royal Warrant. In 1988 we were given the Royal Warrant by Her Majesty the Queen, and in 1995 we received one from the Prince of Wales.

Frank Westwood

Below stairs

I was born in Guildford in 1905 and went to school in Emsworth. I was a scullery maid at Uppark for three years and it was a lovely place to work. The Lord and Lady of the house were Miss Beatrice and Colonel Featherstonhaugh.

I shared a room with another girl right up at the top of the house and we were the first up – at 5.30 a.m. each day. I would come down a winding stairs with a candle and in front of me was the scratch of rats! Of course we didn't have electricity and it was creepy up those blinking stairs. I once saw a blur of someone looking over the banisters: they said it was the ghost. I had a uniform – a blue frock thing, a white apron and a cap – same uniform summer and winter. My first pay packet was twenty-odd pounds for the whole year.

They had a big range with a steel fender and I'd have to get that clean and lay it ready for the cook. I had to clean the copper pots with sand and soft soap, then scrub the big kitchen table, do all the vegetables and maybe skin a

Reg and Violet Sherrington of 6 Cardew Road, Liss, June 1988.

dozen rabbits or partridges; a man used to come from Emsworth and he'd give me a penny per skin. I used to have to pluck rooks but there was only one part of the rook that they ate! Then I'd help dust in the drawing room, do the open fireplace and scrub the scullery and the passages. It was cold down the passages in the wintertime. The path that goes from the larder to the house is made of deer bones. Miss Beatrice used to be terrified of fire; she only had to smell anything and she'd come down the long staircase and say, 'Violet, is there something burning there?'

Violet Sherrington
[Uppark burnt down in 1989! – P.P.]

Garden boy

I was born in 1904 at West Harting in The Greyhound public house and people used to say, 'that's a good place to be born!' I went to school in Harting and started work as a garden boy at Uppark in 1918 when I was fourteen. I didn't live in, I lived down in the village so I had to walk up that hill every day for six-and-a-half years. I got nine shillings a week. In the end I had three cousins and a brother working at Uppark.

My first duties included watering the plants in the greenhouses; they had a melon house, a peach house and five vineries. The head gardener was a lady; her husband had to go to the 1914 war and he got killed early on and she was there for perhaps a year or so and then the poor woman died. Her father used to be head gardener and his name was Gale. They then got another gardener named Smith and he was there a few years. Come Saturday, I used to have to ask him if I could go off to play football for the village.

We used to start at seven and work till five with half an hour for lunch and an hour for dinner. Saturdays was up to four. We took our own sandwiches but we used to have our lunch at 9 a.m. because we started so early in the morning and we were ready for it. I'd go into the larder where Barford the footman was and we used to sit up in the corner with the old fire and go to sleep.

We grew all our plants from seed and we'd grow a few bananas up there but they weren't big, as we couldn't get the heat. When I started I used take a barrel load of apples a day to the house and every afternoon I used to take the dessert fruit down. We had dry summers in those days and the head gardener used to say 'go home at dinner time and come back in the evening to water', but we wouldn't get any extra. The water for the hot pipes was heated by wood, and there were two furnaces – you could get inside of them, they were like the old steam engines; they used to get so much tar from that wood. The head gardener had to keep the fire going all night.

I left Uppark because of the money. We didn't get much money in those days – even after the last war I only got £2 a week, but they were happy times.

Reginald Sherrington

Carpenter

My father's trade was estate carpenter but in those days you were expected to do everything you were asked. One day in 1926, the year of the Great Strike, the rain was coming and the hayrick was exposed so they got a heavy tarpaulin to cover it. My father was told to help but in doing so he had a hernia and had to go into hospital. He got compensation but he wasn't able to do heavy work again so he bought this 'Tin Lizzie' – a little car with a fabric top – I think it was a Ford. He was taught how to drive by a man called Chowny and he set up this taxi business from The Square to Froxfield. He used to be quite busy; it was more like a little bus route than a taxi. When he gave up the taxi business

we moved away to Bentworth, near Alton, where he took on the job of carpenter and electrician on the Burkham estate of General Sir George Jeffries. One night in 1932, he went out on a motorcycle, got thoroughly wet, got pneumonia and died. I was eighteen years old.

Earnest Foard

Child's

I left school when I was fourteen and went to work at Child's, the stationers and booksellers in Petersfield High Street. There was the printing press at the back which used to produce the *Hants and Sussex News,* otherwise known as The Squeaker.

June Edwards

Petersfield blacksmith

I came to Petersfield when I was about four and I'm now seventy-four. I was commissioned in the Royal Engineers and during my National Service I served in Egypt and Kenya. When I was in Kenya I wrote to my parents saying that I would need a job when I got home. My parents wrote back saying that the old blacksmith in Petersfield, Joe Smith, needed an assistant and so I replied saying that if he'd have me I would be happy to work for about six weeks – and here we are, fifty-four years later!

He was getting on even then so I did most of the work but he was a very powerful man and was the sparring partner of Joe Becket, the professional boxer. He retired when he was eighty-six and handed over to me but I still trade as Joe Smith because he said, 'I have no children and when I pack up it would be nice if my name could go on', so I said, 'By all means, I'll trade as Joe Smith'. Mr Smith used to go out at 6 a.m. to the various farms to shoe

Blacksmith Steve Pibworth in his forge, Petersfield, 2003.

the horses before they went out; we used to have some horses come to the forge and they would be a damned nuisance because they would turn up just before lunch and it didn't do to leave them. I didn't pretend to be, or have the desire to be, a farrier but I can do pretty well anything anybody wants in the steel line. I have excellent friends and sub-contractors and between us we can take on anything – that is if I like the look of the people. If I don't then I say we're too busy! Which is fun because it gives us a sense of power!

We keep on getting people saying, 'You ought to turn this place into a museum', and I tell them that when I went into the eighteenth-century plumber's shop at the Weald and Downland Museum at Singleton it was just like going into my own forge! Some of our tools are well over 100 years old but we use them still.

Richard Mason and Leigh Richards are my present assistants. They have both been with me since they left school – Richard for twenty

years and Leigh for fifteen. Before that I had Rob Dimmock for twenty-five years; he left me ten years ago but we are still great friends and he has got his own forge up at Froxfield. I try to bring Richard and Leigh in and get their thoughts and ideas on jobs and very often they come up with something interesting – we work as a team. I am the designer and I deal with the customers and leave the boys to work without interruptions, which is how they like it. I have a good eye for what looks right; I spend many weekends in London just taking in the wrought iron design and I often pop into the V&A because they've got a very good wrought iron gallery. Generally speaking, if I'm happy with it, the client is also.

When I started at the forge a contractor came in wanting some angle irons, about sixteen of them, all 9ft long. He had a nice new car and when he went to get them in they wouldn't fit so, to our amazement and consternation, he just smashed them through the back window! He said, 'Don't worry. I've

The forge, Petersfield.

got sixteen men waiting for work and the window will only cost £20 to replace'.

On 23 November 2002 we were unloading a 40ft girder. We had three people holding one end and the other end was resting on a trestle and, for some unknown reason, the girder slipped to the side of the trestle and tipped it up and the girder fell down. The driver and one of the boys let go but Leigh held on and the girder took the top of his fingers off. That was awful, but it is the only accident we have had in fifty-four years and we have now devised a special trolley to prevent it happening again.

Steve Pibworth

Brickworks

North Stroud Lane is where the brickworks and the brick workers' cottages were built in the nineteenth century. The Common was wooded and the land is made up of very wet clay with underlying sand and is consequently hard to farm. However, with clay and sand you get bricks and that is the reason for the brick and tile industries that grew up within Stroud. My grandfather, George Penn, used to quarry the sand and then transport it to the brickworks by horse and cart. They started to make bricks and tiles on a large scale in the late 1800s but the deeds of my house, which is built on an old sandpit, show that the first licence was issued to a John Robynet in 1571 and the last licence for the quarry on our land was 1894. The industry died out in the 1950s and I believe the Gammon family were some of the last families to be involved in the making of bricks in this area.

Clinton Brown

Milkmen

My father came back from the war in 1919 and when a farmer died he took on Fern

George Penn and baby Len Penn, c. 1906. George used to transport the sand to the brickworks.

Cottage Farm (on the Longmoor Road). Horses and carts, which were used to transport the stones for the making up of roads, was the main income for of the farm, but that died out when lorries took over, so my father ended up with just the milk and a vegetable garden.

He used to deliver milk locally. He carried it in a proper milk pail and when he had plenty he'd give them good measure, but when he was short they just got the measure they asked for. Somebody put their jug out and said, 'That's not a pint Mr Gilburd'. He said, 'It is'. 'No it isn't', came the reply. So he tipped the milk back into the pint measure and the rest that was left in the jug was tipped back into the pail – she had been given well over a pint, but because she was used to a generous 'pint' she thought she hadn't got her full share.

Norman Gilburd

Milk factory

I left school in 1941 and my first job was with the 'milk factory'. South Eastern Farmers was formed in 1923 and was based in the old Drayton Hotel, up by the railway station. It later became the United Dairies. We used to go round the farms and pick up the milk in ten-gallon churns and put it on lorries to take to the dairy. As you can imagine, that was quite a weight for a fourteen-year-old but we developed a special way to pick them up, there was a knack to it. Once it was in the dairy it was pasteurised and then put into tankers and sent up to London.

Geoffrey Gard

Artificial inseminator

After the Second World War, my father, Frank Brown, stayed in Petersfield and married my

Geoffrey Gard in the Petersfield Museum, 2003.

mother. Charlie Musselwhite, one of my mother's cousins, was farming Mount Pleasant Farm when he heard that there was a job going at a new company that was setting up in Petersfield. My father applied and became an artificial inseminator for the Hampshire Cattle Breeders, a job he did up until he died in 1971. The Cattle Breeders yard and office are now under housing on Princes Road. As a small boy I used to go out with him to the farms, with the canisters of liquid nitrogen in the back of the little Mini Travellers they all used, and I learnt all about country life.

Clinton Brown

Mr Brown

Some of the farming community,
Has just lost a good friend;
Mr Brown from the AI Centre:
Is no longer around.

Death took him suddenly, last month,
And we all personally mourn;
Because one good man,
From this life has been shorn.

We will no longer see,
That happy face;
Through all the years
That smile has been in place.

Through sunshine and showers,
Snow, mud and gales!
Frost and cold;
That smile it would hold.

A fractious heifer;
An awkward cow:
He was gentle and patient,
There was never a frown.

He has called at the farm,
Through nearly sixteen years;
We will never forget him,
We have all shed a few tears.

'Brownie' has gone –
But, his smile lingers on.

B.J. Doherty

Sheet post office

I ran the Sheet post office from my home for twenty-one years, until I was about seventy. People came straight in the door and into the sitting room where I had a simple table as a counter. After a year, Norman built a little annex onto our house especially for the post office and both my home life and working day became much easier. Before the annex was built I would find people wandering through the house! As a service to the community I used to display the work of local artists and potters and sometimes sell it for them. I also sold basic foodstuffs on behalf of the council.

Frank Brown (father of Clinton), second on the right, was the artificial inseminator for the Hampshire Cattle Breeders. (Courtesy of Donald C. Eades)

We had no adding machines in those days but I was usually very accurate. I was worried when decimalisation was introduced – I thought I would never learn it but I soon did. I saw lots of different stamps over the years. The college boys would come in and look for mistakes: I would give them the whole sheet to go through and they would want the one right in the middle! If they found one with a mistake they would get money for it.

Phyllis Gilburd

Rowland Son & Vincent

My great-grandfather, Charles Rowland, came up from Cornwall in the 1880s and worked for a company called Gammon Brothers, a gentleman's outfitters. We think that he was made manager in about 1882, so we now say that we were established from that date. He had five children – my grandfather William and four daughters – and when grandfather was old enough, he went into the business. By this time my great-grandfather owned the shop and he called it Rowland's. When grandfather went into it, it became Rowland & Son. During the First World War, my grandfather went to Nottingham to work in ammunitions and when he came back he had a daughter, Beryl, my mother. She married Percy Vincent, a cabinetmaker, in 1934 and grandfather invited him to join the company – so we became Rowland Son & Vincent. The shop gradually evolved from being a gentleman's outfitters in the 1940s to selling furniture and furnishings after the war. Now we do mostly upholstery and hardwood furniture: we don't do a lot of fabrics these days. We are the oldest business in Petersfield. My brother David is Marketing Director, Michael is the Managing Director and I am in charge of the funeral side. I have been working in the firm for fifty years.

Mary Vincent

Laying out

I used to go and lay people out when they died. I always used to say: 'Respect the dead, because they are beyond you'. I always felt I was helping somebody and that is what kept me going. I never got depressed or frightened.

June Walker

Funeral directors

I used to help out on the funeral side of the business and in the early 1980s, The National Association of Funeral Directors were tightening up the rules and regulations so they suggested I went for the diploma. I soon found I was working until seven or eight o'clock at night; I'd then come back and do Rowland's books. Eventually I went full time on the funeral side and I've been doing that for the last twenty-odd years. Now my niece, Marsha Vincent, is coming into the company; she will be third generation on the funeral side.

We started funerals because dad wanted to do curtain making and fabrics, which they didn't do in the 1930s, but grandfather said, 'No,' so dad said, 'Well in that case I'll do funerals.' A few days later someone came in and asked him to do a funeral. Father said, 'I didn't know what to do but I muddled through!' You see we had a workshop which provided the cabinetmakers for making the coffins, upholsters for lining the coffins and staff for carrying the coffins; this is how a lot of funeral businesses started. Builders also used to do funerals because they also had the workshops and the staff – there used to be Moulds, Barnes, us and two others – five funeral firms in the town between the 1930s and the '50s (we pooled our resources during the war). After that, until August of 2003, we were the only funeral directors in Petersfield, but now Michael Miller, who worked for us for some twenty years, is managing another

one in the High Street. June Walker, Betty Salisbury and Mrs Boswell did the laying out of the bodies for us but now we use a professional embalmer. We have just one hearse and we hire the limousines; the difficulty comes when we have Romany funerals because they want about twenty-four cars – the gypsies have large extended families and they all want to travel in the limousines.

A very well-known Petersfield environmentalist would go round the town picking up cans and paper and would stand in the middle of the High Street and cough when a car went past! When she died we had to get her a special horse and cart. Michael Miller conducted the funeral and he had to walk from the church to the cemetery in front of the horse – he said it was nerve-wracking because as he was walking down the High Street all he could hear was 'clip, clop' – and it seemed to get closer!

In a survey of the South of England, Petersfield citizens came out as the longest living. We live until our eighties or early nineties: in fact centenarians are almost quite common.

Mary Vincent

Grocer

I learnt my trade at George Bailey's fruit shop on the corner of Chapel Street. We couldn't handle fruit until we had been there nine months, we could only serve vegetables. We were well trained in those days and when I go into the supermarkets now, I nearly go mad at everybody squeezing the fruit. Bailey's owned the gardens opposite the cinema in Swan Street and we used to go and cut big bunches of black grapes with the 'film' on them. We had lychees and avocado pears and that sort of thing; they make so much fuss now but we had all the exotic fruits in those days. I worked for Bailey's until I got married to Harry. He was a cabinetmaker at Rowland Son &

Above: *Nancy de Combe outside The Fruit Basket, St Peter's Road.*

Right: *Margaret Childs, 2003.*

Vincent's and ended up on the funeral side. I lost him eighteen years ago. After the war I went back to Bailey's and then I had my own fruit shop, The Fruit Basket, next to where we lived in St Peter's Road. It's a flower shop now.

Nancy de Combe

Telephonist

I worked as a GPO telephonist at Petersfield from 1941-48 before being promoted to instructor at our training school in Aldershot for a year, and then I went to Guildford. In 1952 I came back to take charge of the Petersfield exchange and finally I was based in Portsmouth as a Service Rep, retiring from British Telecom after forty-one years' service. When I started my career there were only six telephonist positions and a supervisor but when I finished there were more than twenty telephonists, plus two supervisors. Petersfield was an extremely busy manual exchange.

One wasn't allowed to listen to conversations but occasionally you had to listen to see that people got through to the right number. On one occasion, a lady had had trouble getting through so we rang her number for her. She wanted to book two seats for something but when she asked there was a silence and then they said, 'Madam, who do you think you are talking to?' and she said the name of one of the Portsmouth theatres and they said, 'Madam, this is the undertakers!'

We started receiving some obscene phone calls and when the perpetrator was caught he turned out to be an Isle of Wight police officer! He was sent to jail but then the calls started again so we reported it and it was the same policeman – he had been released from jail. The girls were asked if they would be willing to keep these people talking so that they had time to trace the calls. Kids used to do it during the holidays but the local policeman would catch them and march them home to be told off by their dads.

Christmas day was a lovely day to work because everyone was happy. Boxing Day was a horrible day to work because everyone was bad tempered! One Boxing Day, a customer rang up wanting to know how to play a particular new game, which I'd heard of but knew nothing about; he really tore me to pieces because I couldn't tell him how to play it!

Margaret Childs

Teacher

I taught in the little St Peter's Road school. It was at the time of the 1956 Hungarian uprising and they brought about a dozen Hungarian children to Petersfield. They didn't speak a word of English and we didn't speak a word of Hungarian but we got on famously. I remember one very distinctly – a true Hungarian gypsy type with big earrings and plaited hair. They stayed with us for about four months before returning to their families. I had a letter from one, thanking me for looking after his smaller brother. They were nice children but they squabbled between themselves and I had no idea what they were on about!

Irene Chapman

Coronation dinner

I waited at tables for the celebration dinner of the Coronation of King George VI at the Town Hall because, in my spare time, I worked for Mrs Hall's caterers in the High Street. It was on Wednesday 12 May 1937. Local people provided the entertainment: Mrs Finch was on the violin, Mrs Whitehead the cello, Mrs Peters, Theodora Wassell and Lynda McCallum on the pianoforte and Mr Percy Vincent was the singer. There was even a 'humorous programme' with Ronald Yates and Harry Powell doing funny turns – Mr

Petersfield telephone exchange, c. 1947.

Bennett and Mr Kemmish accompanied them on the piano. George Bailey gave the welcome address and the Reverend Kent (Rural Dean and Vicar of Petersfield) said the Grace. The food looked wonderful: roast sirloin or roast stuffed lamb with spring cabbage and new potatoes followed by trifle, cheese and biscuits and tea.

Nancy de Combe

Milk boy to butler

I was born at 14 Sussex Road, Petersfield, in 1904. Sussex Road was originally known as Golden Ball Street because of the pawnshop on the corner. At 10 years old I worked, morning and evenings for the Misses Lucas at the top of Borough Hill and as I got older I did a paper round for Mr Bradley at the corner of Lavant Street, both jobs were hard work for someone of my age. Thank God those days of exploitation are over for the young ones of today.

Eventually I was taken on as 'milk boy' to Mr Sam Hardy, the Petersfield Squire and Master of Foxhounds. I used to go up to Fairfield Farm to collect the milk, eggs and butter and take them to The Spain by 7.30 a.m. On Saturdays I would help in the kennels that were at the back of the Jolly Sailor pub in the Causeway. Mr Hardy had a pack of mixed dogs and I would help Mrs Smith, the kennel woman, to scrub out and renew all the straw in their beds. I would wash all their collars and leads in soft soap and polish the brass buckles. Sometimes I would be allowed to exercise the dogs in the field opposite the kennels. I would also light up the big copper ready to boil the horseflesh that came for the dogs. Walter Bone looked after the dogs; he would take them out in the meadows for exercise and sometimes the poor old chap would get tangled up in their leads! If we happened to see this we would have a good laugh, which didn't go

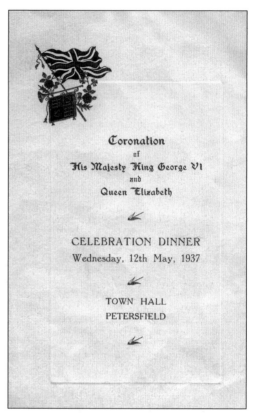

Coronation
of
His Majesty King George VI
and
Queen Elizabeth

CELEBRATION DINNER
Wednesday, 12th May, 1937

TOWN HALL
PETERSFIELD

Nancy de Combe's coronation dinner programme, 1937.

down well with Walter. He had a shepherd's van in which he slept, also a building with a little kitchen range to do his cooking. My boss was a great cigar smoker so I used to save all the butt ends for Walter, who would cut them up to smoke in his pipe. In those days the cigars were sent down from London in lovely cedar wood boxes, each cigar costing about 5s.

Just before the end of the first war Mr Hardy asked Mum and Dad if they would let me join his household staff as a trainee footman. I was taken by Mr Chambers, the butler, to the local tailor and was fitted out with a blue suit (my first long trousers), white shirts, black ties, black patent shoes and black socks. I went down to Sussex Road to see Mum, feeling grand in my new rig-out but also very homesick. Mr Hardy was considered

Harry Walter Edwards, footman to Sam Hardy, pictured aged fifteen in 1919.

as a man with plenty of money, although my pay was only 5s a week but of course my food and clothes were provided so I suppose it wasn't too bad. Eventually I qualified as a footman so that meant a trip to the boss's London tailor. My formal uniform consisted of black doe-skin trousers, red waistcoat, dark green coat with thirty-two brass buttons, each with the family crest (a sort of dragon's head); shiny, stiff white collar and a white bow tie. For the mornings I wore a double-breasted blue suit, white shirt and a black tie.

Puppy shows were held at the kennels at Droxford and a lunch would be laid on for those farmers whose ground was hunted on during the winter. It was a grand affair held in a huge marquee, seating about 100 people. Caterers did the food and Mr Chambers and I

served a champagne cup which we made up, and believe me it was good – some of the farmers didn't know whether it was Christmas or Easter!

Mr Hardy entertained during Goodwood race week. There was a large store by the farm entrance, which was about 70 ft x 20 ft, which was thoroughly cleaned and prepared for a ball. The florists would be called in and the place transformed. After dinner, the guests would walk through a covered walkway from the house to the store where there was an orchestra for the dancers. The staff would serve all sorts of food after midnight and the butler and I had to open bottles of champagne in the butler's pantry; we had to have the window open as the corks went off like a gunshot – the following morning the gardener had to use his wheelbarrow to collect all the corks from the lawn.

We used to say amongst ourselves that the boss was dotty because you would hear him singing whilst dressing in the morning and then suddenly he would start swearing and shouting that 'nothing would bloody fit' and he was a 'poor unfortunate so-and-so', then out would go the offending garments through the window! When things had calmed down, I would go out and collect everything up. He had many scarlet coats and his riding boots had special tops which were cleaned with a powder (just damped), but I was not allowed to do that – Mr Chambers did the tops and I did the boots with Day and Martin's polish, which was like black lead and damned hard to get a shine from.

I was getting on for twenty years old and I wanted a change but the butler persuaded me to stay, as he knew things weren't too healthy with the boss's money affairs. During that year Mrs Hardy had a son, Charles, but I'm afraid things didn't improve for Sam Hardy and he lost a great deal of money on the Stock Exchange. It all ended with the staff being given a month's notice. The butler and I were

Harry Edwards with the Hambledon Hunt.

lucky, as Mr Hardy's brother, who lived in Cheshire, wanted us to work at his house. Fred Hardy was a well-known Manchester brewer who owned Hardy's Crown Brewery.

Later I moved down to Buriton where I was Butler to Colonel Algernon Bonham-Carter for twenty-eight years.

Harry Edwards

4 The War Years

Seaforth Highlanders

I was a Boy Scout and we happened to be assembled on the Petersfield Square one morning when the Seaforth Highlanders marched into town. Each of us Scouts was detailed to march the different groups to their billets. I can still hear those big brawny Scots saying, 'A little child shall lead them'. I had to take one lot to a Mr Stubbington's, to a house just above ours in Sussex Road. The eight soldiers had a big room which had been cleared of furniture, so they just put their own blankets on the floor to sleep on and they got their food from their own canteens. We took our trek cart out with a gramophone to Heath Lodge in Sussex Road, which had been turned into a military hospital, and there we would play records to the soldiers who were recovering from their wounds. They made a great fuss of us. They had a great time before being sent overseas. One New Year's Day, a Scot's Glengarry was stuck on William of Orange's head, an empty whisky bottle slung around his neck and a turnip stuck on the scroll he had in his hand. I'm sorry to say that only a few came home from France and all their officers were killed at Mons. The First World War came to an end, much to the rejoicing of everyone, and one thing amused me that day: the gas lamp in the alley wasn't lit of an evening when all the other lights were back on, so some brainy bloke climbed up the lamp post and put up the following notice: 'The Lord said "Let there be light", so for Christ's sake, lets have some!' That did the trick!

Harry Edwards

The Black Watch

I was born in Southsea in 1907, moved to Liss Forest when I was two and stayed until 1916 when my father, Harry, was called up, and then we moved to Longmoor. When the First World War started, I remember going to the end of our road to watch the soldiers go by. We had six of the Black Watch billeted on us in one room. My mother said, 'We can't take six, we've only got one room,' but the Sergeant looked at the room and said, 'Oh yes, plenty of room for six, clear it out!' I spoke to them but had a job to understand them because they were real Scots. They stayed with us until they went to France and then we had letters from them, but I know four of them were killed, and I think the fifth one was, but I don't know anything about the sixth.

Norman Gilburd

The Enterprise Tea Shop

My mother ran a small tea shop in Longmoor called The Enterprise Tea Shop. At that time there was a camp opposite our shop, at the top of Longmoor Hill, which we called Apple Pie Camp. Longmoor Camp was further up and one camp was for the road repair people and the other was a railway company. I used to go round with a bath and collect the dirty things and the soldiers used to say, 'Make way for a Naval Officer.' We had to draw all the water up by hand with a bucket from a 60ft well. We would put it in the tin bath and then carry it up to the tea shop. We had a little water indoors but that was rainwater and not fit to drink.

My grandfather used to help. He took my father's job during the war (as bailiff of a small farm) but he came in and helped mother serve. Some soldiers came in and said, 'I'll have a strawberry jam sandwich please.' 'Strawberry jam be damned!' he'd say, 'You'll have what we've got!' My father didn't make any money but mother did because we had lots of trade from the camp that was nearly on the doorstep. They tried to bar the soldiers from coming to our tea shop and force them into using their own canteen, but they used to nip down the footpath to us.

When the 'Charleston' came out we all had a go. All the family came down to the tea shop and somebody came to teach us, after we closed, of course. The man who taught us made a crystal set and that was the first time I heard radio; it was really good. We had to have headphones on of course but if we put the headphones in a bowl we could sit around and we could all hear, though not very well. We heard dance music and news, but when the BBC closed down you could just hear Paris, faintly, or at least that is what we reckon it was! And it was very often I would wake up in the morning with the earphones still on!

Norman Gilburd

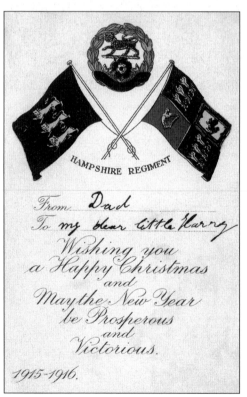

Left: *Hampshire Regiment Christmas card to Harry Edwards from his father, Harry Edwards Sr.* Right: *Harry Gilburd, Norman Gilburd's father, during the First World War.*

Left: Harold Danby, Phyllis Gilburd's father, pictured during the First World War. Right: William Tubbs in 1914. He was Jennifer Robinson's maternal grandfather.

Postcards

When the local lads joined up they gave photographs of themselves to my parents and these were pinned up in the pub. They were continuing a tradition started during the First World War. My mother was a ward maid at the nursing home in Coldhayes and she had photographs of the soldiers she had looked after. When they went to the Front they sent her postcards with lovely messages. All these photographs and postcards from two world wars are very poignant and a terrific slice of history.

Ellen McCutcheon

Banned area

This was a 'banned area' when they were getting ready for the invasion. We didn't know what was going on and the atmosphere was very odd. The train would stop at Haslemere and spend quite a while there and you'd see people being pushed off. The military police asked to see identity cards and if you didn't live within this area they took you off the train and wouldn't let you go any further. Brighton was a banned area and, as my grandmother lived there we couldn't go from our banned area to her banned area so we couldn't visit each other. Midhurst wasn't banned so we were all able to get the bus to have tea with her. Of course the Seawards

63

For England, home and
beauty,
I'll gladly do my duty,
And though with love
I'm yearning,
I soon shall be returning
To her I love the best
of all,
Who gave me up at
duty's call.

Left: *One of the many First World War postcards
sent to Annie May Oakley (mother of Ellen
McCutcheon of the Harrow) while she was working
at Cold Hayes.*

Below: *Cold Hayes Auxiliary Hospital, Liss.*

Opposite: *Margaret Maybrey (née Lee), 2003*

Cold Hayes Auxiliary Hospital, Liss.

weren't bothered because they never went out of Petersfield anyway!

Charles Hardy

Water tank

There was an enormous round water tank in The Square, in case of fire. It was at least five feet high and about twenty to thirty feet across – we used to run round it. It was behind the statue and it seemed to cover practically the whole of The Square. We also had an air-raid shelter to the left side of the church gate. We never used it but it was there for years.

Margaret Maybrey

Blackout

The blackout was quite fun and we weren't afraid to walk about anywhere in the dark. I once dropped my handbag in Chapel Street and it went down with a clatter with all the things spilling out on the pavement, but

people gathered round and some had matches and someone else had a torch and they gathered it all up and put it back in my handbag.

Phyllis Gilburd

The American camp

I was on my horse at the top of Stoner Hill, beyond Froxfield, when I jumped through a hedge and came into the middle of an American camp! We had stacks of Canadians but there weren't any Americans in the town. They came rushing up to me and told me not to tell anybody they were there. They had tents and were gathered around a fire. There were no War Department notices or anything. I didn't tell. The Petersfield people didn't know the Americans were all up on the hill!

Charles Hardy

Workhouse bomb

During the war we lived in two houses in Love Lane while our new house was being built. We had just moved from the second house when a German aircraft came over and dropped a bomb on the workhouse, which was opposite us. It killed the workhouse Master and blew the roof off the house we had just left! I was away from school at the time and could have been in my bedroom so I was very lucky. I was talking to my school colleagues afterwards and they had heard the plane, and Tom Bates (now a retired West Harting farmer) said he had been looking at the plane and Mr Cottle had said, 'Bates, haven't you ever seen a plane before?' and with that there was a huge explosion and the windows were blown out! When we were in our new house I remember looking out of the window and seeing a thousand-bomber raid go over, which was quite something. They just kept coming and coming.

Steve Pibworth

The floors moved

When the bomb landed on the workhouse my mother was putting out the washing in the garden when she saw this stray go over, and then she heard a great thud. At that time my brother was at Churcher's College and she knew it was over that way so she was quite worried. Happily, he later came home from school on his bike. I was taken over to the workhouse after it happened; it was awful. The floors were beginning to move so my father stopped us from going any further. I don't know why we went up there – curiosity I suppose.

Margaret Maybrey

Wrought iron

During the war we had to collect scrap and wrought iron for Spitfires. On Sussex Road there is a big house where diplomats used to live, which had lovely railings. One day the gypsies came with their oxyacetylene cutters and started to cut them but the whole thing caught light – the railings were made of some special hard wood and painted to look like wrought iron! So those remained and later we made some gates for them, which are still there.

Steve Pibworth

Petersfield post office

They called me up during the war and directed me into the Petersfield post office. I worked there for a year, until the end of the war. I took in everybody's parcels to their men and they used to come and say to me, 'I've put this, that and the other in there, what shall I put down on the label to say what it is?' and I used to say, 'You're supposed to put what's in the parcel' but they said 'I'm afraid it'll get stolen', so I said 'Well just put "soap"!' There was tons of 'soap' posted over there!

Phyllis Gilburd

Rationing

There used to be a wonderful butcher called E.J. Baker where Arnold's is now. He had all his meat and fish out on show and the flies were all over it but nobody minded. At Christmas he had turkeys and pheasants hanging by their necks. Meat was rationed but fish, pheasant, quail and turkey were not, so he'd say, 'Tell your aunt I've got nice plump pheasant if she'd like some'. When I went to Australia people used to say to me, 'Oh it must have been hard with all the food rationing', but quite honestly we all looked healthy and I can't remember anybody complaining about being hungry. Milk was rationed but old Mr Bryant used to deliver the milk with a pony and trap and he'd say, 'Oh, Mrs Hardy, I don't bother with no rationing'. Coal was also rationed but we got the same story from Mr Wateridge the coalman!

Charles Hardy

Wartime Buriton

I was six years old when the Second World War started. My father was in the Special Constabulary and he used to go off every evening. Being in the country we were lucky because we didn't really go without anything. We had chickens, and if we were short of food father would go into the field and pop off at a rabbit. We children used to collect rose hips to make syrup for the babies and our mothers would make jams and things with the Women's Institute.

One day we were all playing in the school field when the teachers suddenly shouted, 'Lay down!' We looked up and there was this enormous flying bomb, one of the silent ones, directly overhead. It crashed into a field but I think the bombers were trying to get the main London-Portsmouth railway line. At the time, our parents were working in the hop fields and they came running down because they thought the school had been hit, but we were all fine.

When I was in the infants' we were told to bring a treasure box with treats in it. Mine was an Oxo tin and mother would put in a biscuit or a homemade sweet and the teacher kept them safe. When there was the threat of an air raid we had to sit under our desks and then we were allowed a treat out of our boxes, so we were always longing for the siren to go!

The Buriton Manor garden normally had flowers in it but during the war it was used for vegetables. It was once plagued with rabbits, so they pumped gas down into the holes and the rabbits were supposed to come out and be shot, but nothing happened and no rabbits came out. Well, some bright spark decided they would light a newspaper and shove it down one of these holes and the whole garden erupted in this mighty explosion! That was the end of the rabbits, and the garden! The fire brigade came out from Petersfield as they thought it was a bomb!

June Edwards

Bombs

We used to have Portsmouth people up to do the hop picking every year. That was their holiday and they thoroughly enjoyed it, but when the war started the Colonel let them have the hop-pickers huts to stay in and there

June Edwards, 2003.

was always dancing, singing and sometimes fights in the pubs at night. A lot of them stayed in Buriton after the war and there are still one or two living here now.

Old Dr Bennion used to live in Nursted House. He was nearly a hundred when he died in 1972. He was a Petersfield doctor and he'd already retired when the war started but they brought him back again. He used to mutter to himself as he came up the path and when he read the lesson at church you couldn't understand a word he was saying!

The lime works was closed at the beginning of the war and then the site was used for bomb disposal. The Bomb Disposal Unit would

Sheila Alder, 2003.

Brylcreem boys

An army officer came into the shop once and said to my father, 'Would you go out on Sundays to the searchlight units around Petersfield to cut the men's hair?' Father agreed and the officer said he would give us a petrol ration and a map of where all these units were. So we took our hand cutters out and gave all the soldiers short back and sides. We would do up to thirty a day. We were paid for the work and we would also take out a little case with things from the shop to sell – Brylcreem and stuff like that. One day, just before the invasion, the army came down from Bordon and commandeered all the hairdressers in Petersfield and we cut the men's hair before they went to France. A lot of them didn't even get done as the queue was gigantic.

When I was sixteen or seventeen, I went down to the drill hall headquarters in Dragon Street and volunteered for the Home Guard. We had different places to guard, such as the Festival Hall, the oil and petrol supply at Churcher's College and the coal depot at the Welcome Inn (which used to be over the railway crossing). There used to be a fire tower on Butser Hill and we would climb up these steps to a little hut and look out for parachutes, though I never saw one. We did our shooting training at Bordon on 0.303 rifles. We used to take our rifles and ammunition home with us – a seventeen-year-old with a rifle and live ammunition! I was called up for the Air Force in 1941 and in the meantime my father had to continue in the hairdressing shop as best he could, with his assistant. He was very busy because of the thousands of troops around here, including the Canadians who were camped out at Bramshott Common.

John Freeman

collect the bombs and bring them to Buriton and then let them off in the old lime works – we would hear the bangs. It is said that they would go into the Maple Inn for a drink and the bomb would be ticking away on the lorry! They would bring up to about four at a time and sit on them as they were transported. They must have done something to them to make them safe because the slightest tremor would have set them off. The sailors were all billeted in the village and the lime works was never left unguarded.

Sheila Alder

Mobile perms!

Mr Fleetwood, Jack and my father were called up, so the women had to take over the hairdressing business – Amy (my mother), Auntie Edie, Jack's wife Doris and my older sister Barbara (who had to leave High School early) and several female assistants. At the beginning of the war, 'machineless' perms came out so that the clients could move around if there was an air raid. My grandmother lived with us during the war and she used to put rags in my hair. She put the rag round the end, rolled it up and tied the two ends and I would go to bed with them in.

Margaret Maybrey

Wartime Liss

We moved to Liss in 1938. My father went to work for Sir Hugh and Lady Cocke at Brookdean and we lived at The Lodge for several years. Every Easter they used to close the iron gates at the entrance to the private road to Brookdean, just to prove that it was a private road, but they were melted down during the war for ammunition – so now there are no gates to close! There still isn't a road name up but everyone knows it as Iron Gates Road.

When my father got called up for the Royal Artillery, Grandfather Tubbs came to live with us and took over from my father as

John Freeman, 2003.

Left: *Jennifer Robinson, 2003.*

Below: *From right to left: Jennifer Robinson with their evacuee Anna; Peter Bennett and John Lewis – evacuees with Lady Cocke, Brookdean House, Liss.*

the gardener at Brookdean. He was in the Home Guard but he also did my father's odd jobs for Mrs Bickford-Smith. My mother worked for Lady Cocke but she also worked in the paper mill in Liss; I think they recycled paper to help the war effort. She brought a few books for us to read but they went back again after we'd read them. Lady Cocke went to the village hall and chose Anna, our evacuee.

My sister, Victoria, is twelve years younger than me so I had to look after her. I remember taking her to the village and queuing up for potatoes and sugar when the rationing was on. One day we were coming up Hill Brow when the sirens went and I was so frightened because the bombers were coming over. Liss was targeted at Pophole Farm corner (where the new junior school is now); the device didn't explode but it left a big crater in the road.

We had shelters in the back of the school playground and one day we'd only just got into the shelter in time when a plane came over and machine-gunned the school; we had bullets all down the door! I didn't know at the time that my future second husband was one of the boys in that shelter!

Lord Haw-Haw said on the wireless that the Germans were going to bomb Durford Wood because they thought there were troops in there. We had Italian prisoners working in the woods by Brookdean and when the Canadians came through the village they threw pennies over to the children in the playground. A lot of the village girls got off with the Canadians – I think there are a few Canadian babies grown up now!

Jennifer Robinson

No wine!

We didn't actually have evacuees but family friends who came from London – Jean, Betty and Sheila Reynolds and their mother Ada. The three girls went to Steep School. We also had Grandad (William) Oakley with us, so where they all slept I don't know! There was a woman called Madame Maze, who lived at Steep House (now a nursing home). During the war she opened it up to some French people who had escaped across the Channel. I think she was famous in Paris; one of her relatives was Paul Maze who taught Churchill to paint. They used to come to the Harrow to drink. Of course we didn't keep wine because it wasn't drunk here in those days but we had Sauterne, a very sweet wine, and the French drank that! We kids used to play darts with them; we learnt to score in French as well as the odd swear word but apart from that we never spoke in French. Beer was rationed during the war and we had to get our supplies from Gales, the brewery in Horndean, you were only allowed to have a certain amount so for two or three days a week we were sold out and we had to close the pub.

Ellen McCutcheon

Harrow Lane crash

I used to spend a terrific amount of time fishing on the Heath. In the mornings we used to see the Germans coming over: there would be about twenty in formation and they used the Heath to get their bearings. Occasionally we would see our Hurricanes and Spitfires engage in a dogfight and sometimes one would come down and we would get all excited. One day we were playing in the garden in Sheet and a Spitfire (or Hurricane?) came very low and then we saw a parachute with a man hanging from it. It came down in Harrow Lane so we rushed up there, only to find that the pilot was dead.

Steve Pibworth

Secret testing

A prototype airplane, a secret one they were testing, crashed in Harrow Lane and my father was called out to help with the rescue. An airman had ejected but his parachute hadn't opened and he got caught in the chestnut tree in front of the vicarage, and sadly he died. My brothers nipped up to get bits of metal from it, as treasure, but the authorities had sealed off the whole road from one end to the other while they picked up every bit of metal. If you wanted to go to Petersfield you were escorted through the field – now there is just a brick wall where the plane crashed.

Ellen McCutcheon

Beekeeping

I kept bees for fifty years. First I kept them at home but a neighbour got stung and he said if he got stung again it would be pretty serious, so I moved them up to Bedales and kept them there. A lady up there also kept bees so we amalgamated and ran them between us. We sold the honey for 2s per pound – I didn't make money out of it but it paid for the stuff I bought for the bees. When sugar was on ration I could get a good lot for the bees; they fertilise all the fruit and things so everyone was anxious to keep the bees going.

Norman Gilburd

Farewell father

I went out to Australia with my mother in 1931, when I was just four years old. We left from Tilbury Dock on a miserable day and I said goodbye to my father – I wasn't to see him again until I was seventeen as the war interfered and he advised my mother to keep me out there; we came home just before the end of the war. When we got to Liverpool my father was there with his dog and he was the only one allowed onto the dock. I got on very well with him, even though we hadn't seen each other for thirteen years, as we found we liked the same things – dogs and horses.

Charles Hardy

Club for the soldiers

Mrs Money-Chappelle (known as Madam) ran the Petersfield School of Music and Drama and she had a sort of club for soldiers who were at a loose end. They could come in and get a pie and tea or coffee, and I helped by making the tea or washing up. We used to go and eat in the soup kitchen, which everyone did, to supplement our food rations.

Phyllis Gilburd

Airspeed

Dad wasn't actually called up but they sent him down to Airspeed's in Portsmouth, Hayling Island and Christchurch. Airspeed's made gliders and the wooden planes, such as Dakotas, and some of his gliders landed in Normandy on D-Day.

Mary Vincent

The doodlebugs

When the doodlebugs were about we were still living with my godparents at Borough House. The doodlebugs would come from the Midhurst direction and my bedroom faced that way, so I used to lie on the edge of my bed watching them. They weren't very accurate; those that came over Petersfield were meant for Portsmouth and I knew that so long as there was a flame and they went 'pop, pop, pop', like an old bicycle, we were safe. When the flame went out that meant that they were going to land and we might be for it. I once saw the flame go out so I went straight into my mother's room to wake her up but by the time I'd done that the bomb had landed. The whole house shook, the pictures fell off the walls, the heads of stags and foxes all fell down and the Seawards' collection of cuckoo clocks all went off together. Alice, their maid, came up the stairs (immaculately dressed in her little cap), and said to my mother, 'Mrs Seaward says there has been an occurrence!' Well, we all knew that by then! Mrs Seaward said, 'Well, I think we'd all better have a gin', but I was given ginger ale.

Charles Hardy

Oi! Harry!

Our staff went off to the war one by one and, happily, they all came home safely. Harry de Combe, a cabinet maker, was in the Territorial Army so he went off very early on and was one of those who came back from Dunkirk; Ron Collins, also a cabinet maker, was one of the first to cross the Nile in his tank – he watched some of his mates sail off down the river in their tank but fortunately they got rescued. Harry Brooker, a salesman, went into the postal service because he wasn't fit for combat, but he and Monty were 'like that'! The post office personnel often found themselves behind enemy lines, so it wasn't as safe as it was made out to be. Harry was a very dapper and proper man who lived with his sister. After the Normandy landings some of the local lads were travelling along a Normandy road in a lorry when they saw this chap walking ahead of them. 'I'd know that walk anywhere!' one of them said. The lorry pulled up beside him and he said, 'Oi! Harry!' Harry looked round and said primly, 'Do I know you?' Would you believe it, in Normandy, in the middle of a war!

Mary Vincent

Churcher's College

I was at Churcher's Preparatory School when the war started. We had trenches with corrugated iron over the top and earth over the top of that. We all had to take a little tin, mine was a Horlicks tablets tin, and in it had to be cotton wool to put in your ears and a piece of India rubber to put between your teeth! Can't think why!

One day we were going to school when we heard a sound like a machine gun coming from Sheet Common. A school had been evacuated there and that afternoon Churcher's were playing them so we saw where the machine gun bullets had hit the wooden steps leading up to the cedar hut; it was quite alarming. There were a lot of wooden buildings there and I imagine the Germans thought it was an army camp. I don't think anyone was hurt.

Steve Pibworth

Evacuees

It was the summer holidays just before the war started and we were all thirteen or fourteen. There was Margaret, the eldest, and then John and I, who were twins. It was our job to bicycle around and deliver notes to the people who were to receive evacuees. The notes were printed cards and they said 'Prepare to receive two boys, one girl' or whatever it was. Some of the well-to-do families along the London Road and around Hill Brow were living in very large houses but they were not at all keen about giving up some of their space to poor children from Portsmouth or London, some possibly with nits! The billeting officer had already been around so they had been forewarned. If they didn't agree – tough! We whizzed up the drives on our bicycles, shoved them in and cycled hell-for-leather down the drive again before anybody opened the door.

When the children arrived they were taken to a hall in Liss where they were seen by the doctors; they all had labels on their coats and little gas masks round their necks. Some of them were just given to a family but some of the hosts and hostesses went down and picked children – sounds awful doesn't it? It must have been terrible if you weren't picked.

Caroline Kennedy

Choir

During the war a Doctor Newell came down from London with boys who had been evacuated from Emanuel School and he started up a choir. We already belonged to a local choir and we sang in the festival every year but we joined his choir as well, and they had marvellous singers. We performed Gilbert and Sullivan and entertained the troops down at Longmoor, at HMS *Mercury* in East Meon and at Petersfield Hospital.

Phyllis Gilburd

Toy service

Canon Morley had a lot of refugee children staying at the rectory in Buriton during the war, and he employed a governess to teach and look after them. I think they were children from the 'better class' of person – those who were away doing war work. He had as many as ten or twelve living in the rectory and on Sunday mornings you would see them walking in a line to the church; they would sit in the front row with the Governess and Mrs Morley. Canon Morley started a toy service, usually on a Sunday afternoon in October, when all the children would take toys to be given to hospitals. I used to take a book but I would read it first! When Canon Morley left that tradition finished.

Sheila Alder

Our evacuee

Bob Gibson was our evacuee. I think he is now a multi-millionaire. He inherited from a distant uncle or cousin in Brazil. He was a brainy chap and we all got on well together.

Steve Pibworth

Interesting times

We had evacuees from Portsmouth at the Buriton village school; they were billeted in the hop-pickers' huts. The teachers then were Miss Pleasant, the head teacher, and Miss Coles. Poor old Miss Coles was trying to teach the infants and she clipped one boy, an

Doctor Newell (left), music master, Emanuel School.

Firemen at the Buriton toy service (notice the toys in hands) in the 1920s or '30s. June Edwards' grandfather, Harry Edwards, is second from the left.

evacuee, round the ear for doing something wrong and the next day the mother came down and beat up the poor teacher. It was all quite interesting to us village children; we hadn't experienced anything like this!

June Edwards

A letter from the Palace!

They billeted these East End people on my father. He was living in this big, six-bedroomed house by himself, with a housekeeper, a cook, a chauffeur and a maid. The housekeeper came and said, 'Mr Hardy I can't stay with these dreadful people in the house,' and my father said, 'Well I can't stay here without you,' so he walked up to the council, chucked the key at them and said, 'Here's the key to my bloody house – take my furniture out and you had better just have it, because I'm off!' So all the furniture was put in the cottage and the evacuees moved into Hardy House. That was in 1939 and we didn't get back in the house until 1950; they said the evacuees had nowhere to go! My father consulted solicitors, to no avail. I was then twenty-one and back in Australia, so I wrote a letter to the King explaining that my father, through the kindness of his heart, had given the place to the government (and didn't accept any rental) as part of his war effort, but as it was now almost 1950 I thought he should have it back. I had a nice letter from the King's private secretary saying that he had written to Mr Aneurin Bevan, and if the house wasn't returned within a month, would I write again? Father said he was amazed when he got this letter from Buckingham Palace saying that his house would be returned! He said, 'I've spent so much money on solicitors and you write to the King on a 2½d stamp and get the place back!'

Charles Hardy

Hardy House, 2003.

Triplets

My mother didn't have evacuees at the very beginning, not unaccompanied children anyway, but when the blitz started she had the Jones family from south-east London. The mother's name was Millie and she and mother became great friends. She asked to come to Liss because her husband was a private in the Royal Engineers at Longmoor, so he used to come and see her. They had two little girls, Gloria and Cherie; Millie spelt it 'Sherry'! In 1942 Millie became pregnant and she got larger and larger; her ankles swelled and my mother got concerned about her. The overworked GPs were all doctors nearing retirement and were hanging on 'till the war ended'; there was little antenatal care and no NHS. When Millie was about seven months she went into one of the local maternity homes where she gave birth to unexpected triplets – one of whom had been dead for at least a month!

Caroline Kennedy

An evacuee's tale

In the late autumn of 1939 when I was thirteen years old, my school, Emanuel of Wandsworth Common, was evacuated to Petersfield. We were homesick but we were well treated. There were 600 boys, plus teachers, and we were billeted all around the area. My parents had friends in Petersfield – Mr and Mrs Arnold Arthur Cooper of Bank House – and so our mother arranged for us to be billeted with them. Mr Cooper was the manager of Westminster Bank in The Square and because of his initials we called him Ack-ack!

The Coopers had a son, Dennis, a Cambridge graduate and a conscientious objector. He had a farm up in Harting and so we used to have pheasant and good things like that. During one of the air battles we saw this Messerschmitt 109 out in the distance and it went down on his farm. We raced up there but of course the powers-that-be had already arrived and they kept us at bay; but we could still smell the burning wreckage.

There used to be a gramophone shop at the bottom of the High Street. The lady there was wonderful, though sadly I can't remember her name. We were jazz fans and on Saturday mornings and she would give us records and we would go into cubicles and be there for hours, playing records. We used to buy boxes of needles and the odd record (1s 5½d in those days!). Later, when we moved to Steep, we used to go up Stoner Hill on Sunday afternoons with a portable gramophone and play records – Artie Shaw, Benny Goodman and the rest. We were also allowed to listen to Dennis Cooper's large collection of gramophone records.

My brother and I stayed with the Coopers for about a year but then they had to take a family of evacuees from Portsmouth so we moved to the home of Brigadier and the Hon. Lady Kingsley of Stoner House, Steep. We used to eat in the back with the maids, Rose and May, and it was very much 'upstairs, downstairs'. We used to help the maids clean the machine that cleaned all the knives. One day we'd just finished our lunch when we heard an announcement on the wireless: 'The Admiralty regrets that HMS *Hood* has been sunk' – then only weeks after, they sank the *Bismarck*.

My brother left school and joined the RAF and my friend Vernon Leader joined me at Stoner House. One morning, after a raid, we woke up to find all these strips of silver paper in the garden. They had been dropped to fox the radar – known as window or chaff. Lady Kingsley said, 'You are not to touch anything, the police are coming'.

We shared education and sports grounds facilities with Churcher's but every afternoon we assembled in the main hall when Mr Broom, the Emanuel headmaster, made announcements. Our lessons were held all over the town: we had art lessons with Mr Dixon in the back room of the Sun Inn. It was next door to a little abattoir and you'd hear the poor pigs; we'd also have classes at the Working Men's Institute and the Town Hall. When my brother took his matriculation examination in the Town Hall there was an air raid, so they had to leave all their things and get into a shelter and then carry on again after the 'OK' – very disruptive.

One of the Churcher's boys was a chap named Wright. He had a limp and his medical people said that when he reached the age of twenty-one they'd be able to operate. He was an entrepreneur and one day he bought rolls, put marmite in and sold them to us at ½d each! We loved them so he said he would bring more the next day. I reckon that boy probably owns a chain of supermarkets now – he had vision!

I was in the Junior Training Corps of the Emanuel Officers' Training Corps. Major Hill, our geography master was I/C the OTC and Captain Hipkins, our English master and assistant headmaster, was in charge of the JTC. The cadets would train up on the playing fields. I used to love shooting; we used Lee Enfield rifles with a Morris tube fitted, and .22 ammunition. We were proud to be in the JTC and one day we had some high-ranking chap down from the War Office and we paraded for him in the Town Hall car park; it was a very hot day.

We paraded every Thursday morning between two buildings at Churcher's College and one Thursday there was the groan of an aircraft – it was German, a Heinkel-111, Mark 5a. We heard this sort of whistle and a bomb was dropped. My brother actually saw it; he said it was like a bottle coming out of the aircraft. It hit the workhouse and one of the boys saw a body on a roof. We scattered and threw ourselves down; smoke and the smell of bricks and masonry came across the playing fields – it was very nasty and went on for some time. Of course the whole of Major Hill's lesson was all about this incident; we didn't do any geography!

Malcolm Chandler, pictured just after he joined the Royal Air Force.

Major Hill decided to have an Air Observer Section – we had armbands and anybody who was keen on aircraft recognition could join. We did bouts of an hour each, just walking about with a whistle and looking at the sky, if we saw anything untoward we would blow the whistle and everybody would scatter. One day, one of the boys reported that an RAF aircraft had crash-landed on the road to Stroud. We later cycled out and found that it was a long-nosed Bristol Blenheim Mark 4 which had crash-landed in a field, gone straight across the road and hit a tree. There were long skid marks right across the road and through a hedge and there was an RAF guard on duty.

On Monday mornings we assembled in St Peter's church for a service and directly afterwards we would race down on our bikes to the little barn at the back of the Sun Inn to get our ration of sweets. My brother and I were confirmed at St Peter's on the 7 December 1939, and the Revd Kent took the service. Mother came down.

Malcolm Chandler

Red Cross

The Hampshire Red Cross headquarters was moved out of Southampton before the blitz and spent the rest of the war at the Countess of Malmesbury's home in Hurn. D-Day was launched from Hampshire and the Red Cross had a huge responsibility in getting equipment over to Normandy. My mother was an officer in the Red Cross and, as I was too young to start my nursing training, I worked as a very lowly Red Cross VAD in Wenham Holt – the evacuated home of the Portsmouth Eye and Ear Hospital on the A3. I wore a 'Little Orphan Annie' grey-blue dress and a white apron with a red cross on the front.

Caroline Kennedy

The telephone exchange

Working for the telephone exchange was quite important during the war because we were responsible for giving out air-raid warnings. If there was a purple air-raid warning at night, it meant that places such as the gasworks and ITSIDE had to be warned to close down their fires. We fire-watched on the flat roof of our building every fifth night, all night. I once walked out onto that roof as a bomb was dropped down one of the Buriton searchlights and I was blown right back into the building.

My supervisor gave me strict instructions, which I thought hilarious, on what to do if I saw the Germans coming over the hill. I was given a list of things which I must either destroy or take with me and proceed to the nearest exchange in the direction furthest away from the Germans – if they were coming

Above: *Emanuel boys: Malcolm Chandler is seated, and his friend Vernon Leader is standing, centre.*

Right: *Malcolm Chandler, 2003.*

over Butser, which we could see from our windows – that would have been Liss. The list included such things as files that contained the routing to every exchange in the country and everything that would enable somebody to operate the exchange that had just been vacated, so I suppose it was an important job really.

You could be terribly busy at 5.55 p.m. but at 6.00 p.m. there would be nothing to do because the news would be on, and if Churchill was going to speak the exchange would be absolutely dead.

Margaret Childs

The invasion

My mother and I were sitting in the cottage when Mr Basham came banging on the door saying, 'Mrs Hardy, come quick, it's started – the invasion!' We went out and you literally couldn't see any sky, as there was plane after plane, towing gliders behind. Everybody was gathering in The Square. We knew something was going to happen because for weeks we couldn't get across the Portsmouth Road because of the tanks (you could hear them all night too – they squeaked). I was once on a horse, riding down the High Street and I had to wait for ages but then a kindly military policeman held up the tanks so I could get across. We all knew something was afoot but we didn't know what.

Charles Hardy

It's over!

The day the war finished we went out into The Square and people were doing the Conga and so we joined in!

Phyllis Gilburd

VE Day at Lee Brothers, 13 The Square, Petersfield.

Victory Parade

I didn't go to the school but I did go into the ATC at Churcher's College and, because I was tall, I had to lead the Victory Parade in Petersfield. We marched down the High Street with the army OCTU and Naval schools from Portsmouth and then we formed around The Square. Everybody was there – the ATS, the Land Army and the civilian population of Petersfield were behind us. There was a service of thanksgiving and it was very moving because it was silent; then they blew the 'Last Post', sang 'Jerusalem' and ended up with 'God Save the King' before we marched back.

Charles Hardy

5 Market

Bryant's

I was born in 1917 and came to Petersfield in about 1928. First of all we owned Grange Farm (where Tesco's is now) but we were only there about two years before we bought a fifteen-acre farm in Sussex Road, behind Reeves Removals. Sussex Road used to be called Golden Ball Road because of the pawnshop, so we called it Golden Ball Farm. In 1929 we opened a little shop and sold our produce straight from the farm. It was just a little lean-to on the side of the house and people used to queue up in their cars, even in those days. We reckon that we were the first home produce shop there was and that is how I really started.

Of course we also bought from the Portsmouth market and later on from Covent Garden. We kept twenty or thirty pigs, a few chickens and a dozen or so cows, and from 1930 we had the sole grazing rights on the Heath. Then my brother and I bought Rival Lodge Farm, West Harting, in 1930, we dissolved that partnership and it was then we opened the stall on Petersfield market. We would set up the stall at 5.30 a.m. and have at least a dozen people serving; we were so busy we didn't even know our neighbours. People would go to the pictures and come out at 8.00 p.m. and they would then come to the stall and buy their weekend vegetables – it was a long day.

We've always faced the post office and one day a bull slipped his halter and he more or less backed straight into our stall. He wasn't looking where he was going! The stall went but nobody got hurt. We used to drive our pigs to market, down Sussex Road, over the Causeway, up the school alley, up to the Bell and into the market – five or six at a time. We had all the animals every other Wednesday; that was a good market day because when the farmers had finished their transactions they would buy tons of stuff from us.

The stall got bigger and better and we had more and more customers but then the war came. I joined the army and my stepfather kept the business alive for us. When I came back I bought an old second-hand lorry with some of my war gratuities. We opened up a large shop in Chapel Street and fifteen years ago we opened in Liss and made it our headquarters. In 1962 I bought Gaulds Farm in Greatham and I was there for thirty-two years – our sons, Richard and John, have it now.

We are the oldest stallholders in the Petersfield market by a long way and I worked on it for seventy years – I was about twelve when I started working with my father.

Norman Bryant

'Fishy' Arnett

'Fishy' Arnett sold fish in the market. He came from Portsmouth and was quite a character. If Fishy was nearly sold out he would say 'There you are, there's a haddock

W. Bryant & Sons, Golden Ball Farm, Sussex Road, 1929.

Norman and Ann Bryant, 2003.

The Square on Market Day, c. 1946.

and have this other one for your husband, that'll do him good.' We would go down Saturday afternoons and buy a huge haddock for sixpence and then in the evening the Petersfield Brass Band played, so if you had tu'ppence to put in their hat you had a good day out.

Phyllis Gilburd

A bit of a rogue

'Fishy' Arnett had a market stall long before us but I remember him well. He was illiterate and didn't do scales – he'd sell his fish by 'each', seven for sixpence and things like that. He was a nice fellow but a bit of a rogue. Once he got into trouble with the Weights and Measures people and had a Queen's Council working for him; this QC said what a wonderful man Billy Arnett was and got him off. Anyway, about a year or so later he was in trouble again and when he stood in front of the court this QC, the one who thought he

was a lovely fellow, was against him! He told me, 'One day he was my friend and the next day he was my enemy!'

Norman Bryant

Market lamps

The Petersfield market was the focal heart of the town. London traders came by train and there were several lads, beside myself, who used to go to the station to meet them. 'Carry my bags, boy, and hold my lamp and you'll get half-a-crown' – but we were streetwise and we knew we weren't going to get the half-a-crown; they'd give us a shilling, normally. We carried the bags down from the station to the market and then held their lamps to light the stalls. The lamp was a flare on a pole, I forget if it was paraffin they used.

The well-known George and Jane Puppet Show was very colourful and I think it was based on Punch and Judy. He had a little box arrangement and used to call out, 'All the money I collect today goes to the widows and orphans fund – my old woman's the widow and I'm the orphan!' He used to get quite a lot of children, and even the grown-ups enjoyed it.

In those days the market was big and all the country folk came in for it. We used to get people making cough sweets – they would boil them, make them into slabs and then break them up into little pieces. Another trader sold a corn cure; he had a line of corns in little brass cases on his stall, supposed to be the ones he had cured I think! There was once a big scandal in the town, I forget exactly what it was about, and this man was selling little packets with information about it; I think he was charging sixpence a packet. He was telling people, 'Now, you mustn't open it here.' He sold a lot of them but I was told afterwards that the information was in the newspapers anyway!

I once picked up a bunch of keys in the market so I took them off to the police station and handed them in. Someone claimed them and, as a reward, they took me to the sweet shop in the High Street and they said I could have whatever sweets I liked – I chose some chocolates.

One day, I had done particularly well in the market and I had two shillings to spend; there was a draper's shop just along the road from Lloyds so I went in there and bought a little jersey which was brown with flecks of other colours, a bit like a heather mixture. I was quite smart then.

Earnest Foard

Loose bull

Mr Hunt, the auctioneer, had a fantastically loud voice; we could hear him in our shop. When we were at 17 Chapel Street a bull got loose and came into the shop, and went round the back of the counter. It was jammed in and they had a job getting him out of there!

John Freeman

Earnest Foard, 2003.

Poultry

They started a poultry and rabbits market just round the corner from The Square. I never bought from the market but I sold some once, during the war. I kept chickens because of the fresh eggs; one got ill so I thought I would take it to market as I thought that was the thing to do – but it wasn't at all! The lady that took it rang me up and said, 'This chicken's not well,' so I said, 'I'm sorry, come and get your 3s 6d back,' so she did!

Phyllis Gilburd

Miscellaneous lots

I first came to Petersfield in 1946 when there was still the old-fashioned cattle market in The Square. Harry Jacobs and his father used

Above: *Flora Twort's famous 1933 painting of the old Petersfield Market.*

Right: *The Poultry Market by Flora Twort.*

Both pictures courtesy of the Hampshire County Council Museums Service.

The market, c. 1981.

to auction poultry and also (of particular interest to me) the miscellaneous lots – the odd milk churn, an old plough, a few rakes, spades and things like that. I well remember the broadcaster, Martin Muncaster, doing a piece for the BBC on the closing of the last Petersfield cattle market.

Ken Hick

Future

I think we should have tables on The Square in the summer, so that people can enjoy sitting out and having a drink, as they do on the continent. I also think that all the market stalls should be in the same striped tarpaulins to give a feeling of pride and uniformity. I would like it to look like the French markets, which are superb. Of course it has changed a lot since it was a cattle market, as depicted in the lovely Flora Twort paintings.

Elsa Bulmer

6 Public Houses

The Fighting Cocks

The family of my paternal grandmother, Lucy Annie Edwards, owned the Fighting Cocks pub at 30 Dragon Street, which is no longer there. It was first owned by William Blanchard and then he signed it over to his brother, my great grandfather, Horri Blanchard. The Fighting Cocks became known as the tramps' hotel in the end and became disreputable, so Grandma decided to give it up.

June Edwards

Smuggling!

Mum used to tell us stories of the smuggling that used to go on from the Chichester coastline: in the early hours of the morning Mum would hear someone whistling a short tune and then Grandad Blanchard would clatter down the stairs and meet someone with a horse and trap. Little barrels would be quickly transferred and put in a safe place so that no excise officer could guess where they were – and then everyone went about their everyday work as a matter of course.

Harry Edwards

The Harrow

The Harrow is approximately 400 years old but it has been added to over the years. It was owned by the Church in 1608 and in the nineteenth century the Steep Vestry met here, before the days of the parish council. The public bar is very old: the servery was added on during the First World War and the saloon bar, otherwise known as the smoking room, is probably early Victorian. In the old days they made their own beer and customers took it home to drink. The path at the front was used as a drover's road – it goes to a little stream where they would water their cattle and keep them in a pound overnight and the drovers would get their drinks and food at the pub. The pub is full of interesting mementos – we've still got all the records and the accounts books going back to 1917.

My family came to live in the Harrow in 1926. My parents, Annie May (née Oakley) and Arthur Millington Dodd, met when they were domestic servants at Bedales School; my mother was maid to Mrs Badley, wife of John Haden Badley, the founder of Bedales. When they were first married they rented rooms from the Harrow licensee and in 1930 they took on the licence.

My father was a popular figure (well known for being a ventriloquist) who died in 1958; my mother then took the licence and my two brothers and I helped her run the Harrow until she died; my husband, Edward, who at the time was working as a printer with Thwaites & Watts in Petersfield, became the licensee and when he died in 1999 I became the licensee and now I'm in partnership with my two daughters, Claire and Nisa. In 1990 we bought the freehold and in 1997 we won

FORM No. 71.

4000-6.87.

HANTS CONSTABULARY.

NOTICE
TO
LICENSED VICTUALLERS
AND
RETAILERS OF BEER.

TAKE NOTICE, that if you allow any Police Constable to remain on your premises during any part of the time when he should be on duty, you are liable under 35th & 36th Vict., cap. 94, sec. 16, on conviction, to forfeit for every such offence the sum of TEN POUNDS.

As a general rule, the Hants Constabulary may always be considered on duty when dressed in Uniform.

CHIEF CONSTABLE'S OFFICE,
WINCHESTER.
27th June, 1887.

J. H. FORREST,
Chief Constable of Hampshire.

WARREN, TYP. WINTON.

An amusing old notice from the Fighting Cocks public house, 1887.

Annie May Oakley (later Mrs Dodd of the Harrow) in the window of Bedales School.

Ellen and the late Edward McCutcheon with their two daughters Claire (right) and Nisa (left) outside the Harrow, Steep.

the Good Pub Guide award for Unspoilt Pub of the Year. People say you step back in time when you enter the Harrow; it's an honest-to-goodness country pub, not a tarted-up coaching inn.

I was born in the same room as I now sleep in and my two brothers, Haden, a plumber (named after his godfather, founder of Bedales) and John, a journalist, were born in the room above the public bar. It was great fun being brought up in a public house because there was always something going on. It was probably highly illegal but we kids were allowed in the bar.

I like to think that the poets Edward Thomas and Thomas Sturge Moore and the artist Muirhead Bone came into the pub when they lived in Steep; it has always been a very artistic village. Years ago our customers were mainly farm workers and gardeners but we have lost lots of farms and most of the big estates have gone now.

We've had quite a few famous people in the Harrow. Dame Peggy Ashcroft came in with Sir Alec and Lady Guinness; Jonathan Routh (of *Candid Camera* fame) and John Wyndham (who wrote *The Day of the Triffids*). Lady Guinness was a very good painter and she gave Claire and her partner, Tony Clear, two paintings for doing the flowers for Sir Alec's funeral. When she died, her paintings were sold and all the proceeds went to the McMillan Nurses.

My mother's brother, Jack Oakley, was a well-known character. He had mutton-chop whiskers and always had a twinkle in his eye. He sang country songs and would wear a collarless shirt, a waistcoat (always undone), whipcords, boots, a wide leather belt, a battered trilby hat and he always had a traditional walking stick in one hand and usually a pint in the other! About forty years ago someone took his photo and it was made into a postcard because they thought he was the epitome of a typical English countryman! The postcard is still being sold in the West Country but Uncle Jack didn't get a penny from it; the photographer must have done well out of it though.

Ellen McCutcheon

Uncle Jack Oakley, the archetypal countryman!

A little dog

My grandfather, George Penn, bought the licence of the Harrow public house as a gift for his brother Samuel when he came home from Ypres after having been injured with mustard gas in the First World War. He had the licence from about 1915 to 1924. As a little girl, my mother, Patricia Brown (née Penn) used to visit her uncle at the Harrow to see the little terrier dog he had brought back from Belgium. This little dog had befriended Samuel and his comrades in the trenches and the story is that he used to smell the gas first and let the soldiers know it was time to put their gas masks on – the soldiers would then cover the dog with their greatcoats to protect

him. When Samuel was sent home he brought the dog with him.

Clinton Brown

The bypass

It took seventeen years of bullying and cajoling to sort out the Petersfield bypass – and then there was the battle to get it in asphalt and not concrete. If it had been in concrete it would have been very noisy for everyone living within earshot – and for the Harrow public house it would have been terminal. We had a great campaign to get it changed. I talked to the Department of Transport once a month but they kept giving me wrong costing information, so eventually I went to our Minister and told him about this and he said, 'OK you have your asphalt'. That was about 10.00 p.m. one night but I rang the Harrow and said, 'We've won! It's going to be asphalt.' And the lovely landlady, Ellen McCutcheon, announced it and the whole pub went 'Hooray!'

Michael Mates MP

The Crown

When we stayed with my grandparents, we would sometimes go down to The Crown which was on the corner of Sussex Road and into the back room and have a little drink; the lady who owned the pub at that time was a Mrs Compton and she had a pet pig which she kept in this room. I loved going there because of the pig. Grandmother Lucy ended up in a wicker bath chair because she had very bad legs; I think it must have been arthritis because she'd spent a lot of her life standing on cold stone floors doing washing for other people. She would sit in the chair with a blanket over her and I would sit on her lap and we'd be wheeled down to The Crown where she liked to have a little drop of the hard stuff. She always insisted on giving me a cup of hot milk with loads of sugar in it, but I hated sweet drinks.

June Edwards

The George

A woman played the piano in The George just like Winifred Atwell – she never stopped. She was the wife of the publican and she was known as 'Ginny' because she would say 'Mine's a gin'. All the glasses of gin would be shaking on the top of the piano and you could hear it all around The Square!

The Little Wonder bus sat outside The George and one day my father's cook wanted to go into Harting; she climbed into the Little Wonder with her basket. Old Frank Lambert (the driver, who spent much of his time in The George) came out and she said, 'Be this the bus for Hartin'?' and he said, 'Aye, is', and she said, 'Thank ye very much.' He went back into the pub. Another twenty minutes went by and she was still sitting there with her basket and when he came out again she said, 'When's it goin'?' He said, 'Tomorra'!' The Little Wonder was real private enterprise – just these two buses, which Frank bought cheap after the first war. He didn't know how to mend them and if they broke down he'd tell everyone to get out and walk. He only charged 2d for a single or 3d return. When he first started, Frank said he would go from Petersfield to Harting or East Meon but not Froxfield because 'I don't much like motoring and I don't want to drive up that hill!'

Charles Hardy

Brewery

My father, Fred Tipper, was a drayman for Ameys Brewery before the First World War and was there for years, along with his two other brothers, George and Bill. The brewery was on the corner of Frenchman's Road and Swan Street and is now the Amey industrial estate. Miss Amey owned the place and, although she was a fierce dragon, she always gave us a terrific joint of meat at Christmas and skimmed milk every day of the year; we lived in their tied cottage in St Peter's Road. They used to run out of beer so Dad had to deliver at holiday times and, although he wasn't supposed to take passengers, we used to hide amongst the beer barrels and get a ride to Hayling Island and then crawl out, have an hour or so there when he was unloading, and then get a ride back home.

Nancy de Combe

7 Leisure

'Blooded!'

I had a Shetland pony called Stella when I was two years old and I got up to horses when I was fourteen. I used to hunt and was 'blooded' in the garden of Widow Knight's cottage in Stroud. The poor fox had got into the toilet at the bottom of the garden. I carried the brush home on my saddle and had the mask (head) of the fox mounted on a shield; I had four in the end. People think it is terrible now but I suppose that when you are seven or eight you don't think about it. When the Hardy family lost all their money in 1929 my father lost his job as stud groom and my horse riding came to an end but we kept in touch and remained friends; Mr Hardy came to my wedding.

Nancy Ford

Dances

On Saturday evenings the young people would walk to Steep village hall to a little dance, which cost us sixpence, including drinks (non-alcoholic of course) and a biscuit. Ma Green (her name was M.A. Green) used to play the piano. We moved around in a little gang, perhaps eight of us, and we used to walk to Butser and take a picnic and have a happy time. Sometimes we could afford to go into the restaurant that ran a tea dance, but I think that was a shilling, so we didn't go often.

Phyllis Gilburd

Sheet Troupers

When I was young in the early 1950s the Sheet Troupers would put on an annual production in the village hall. It was a variety act, so anybody who had any talent (or not!) would take part. The whole village would turn out to watch their neighbours performing. I used to do ballet and others would sing, recite or perform their 'party piece'.

Jenneth Seddon

Bell ringing

I have been ringing the bells at St Peter's for twenty years and in the old days we would go all round the churches and go into competitions. My brother, Kenneth Tipper, has been captain for fifty-two years and my husband, Harry, repaired a wheel in the tower. I would still do it if I could go out at night, but you can't go out on your own at night these days. In Buriton, a few years ago, we rang until about 7.00 p.m. A person come charging up and said, 'You should stop these bells!' I opened my big mouth and said, 'Well you shouldn't have come to live under the bells – you're lucky that you can hear them because my deaf grandma is always saying 'I wish I could hear our bells!'

Nancy de Combe

Right: *Nancy Ford, age four, on Stella, her first Shetland pony, 1920.*

Below: *Sheet Troupers. Margaret Childs is seen seated front with a ukelele. Her father, George Childs, is back row, centre.*

Pianola

If Mr Hardy didn't feel like dressing for dinner, he would order a basin of bread and milk and have it in the drawing room, with me playing the pianola. I would put the rolls of music in, then sit on the stool and pedal away. I had a little handle to guide the pointer along the music roll as it unwound, so as to be soft or loud; sometimes I sat there playing the thing for a couple of hours until the boss was ready to go to bed, when he would say, 'That's enough, get my bedtime candlestick,' and off to bed he would go without saying goodnight!

Another of the boss's hobbies was taking a concert party around the villages, sometimes twice a week. He was a great admirer of Sir Harry Lauder; he used to entertain Sir Harry and had his permission to sing his songs. Of course that wasn't enough for the boss, he had to have lovely kilts and jackets with plaid shawls, beautiful stockings and shoes with huge silvery buckles, also the jewelled dagger in the top of the stocking – complete outfits of different clans. He couldn't sing but there were other artists who made up for him! The butler and I used to follow the party around with refreshments. We had a big urn, primus stoves and masses of food, which we prepared before setting out – it was a real palaver. All of it must have cost the boss a fortune but these concerts were all for charity.

Harry Edwards

Splash!

The Petersfield open-air swimming pool originally had only icy cold water. A group of us decided to start a campaign called 'Splash' and eventually we made enough money, with a grant from the Urban District Council, to heat it. I swam the Solent to raise money for it. I was thirty-seven at the time and I trained for a year in the pool. We set off one Saturday and Ken was in the boat to help with the navigation. I was swimming with the tide and had the Gosport Flats and Portsmouth on the horizon when I got as far as the cold water channel (which is almost spitting distance from the Southsea shore) when at that point I went under, unconscious! It was a very cold August and the water was so cold. They dived in, got me out of the water and sat me by the boiler of this little boat and when I'd thawed out they wanted me to go back and complete the 100 yards to the coast but my husband wouldn't allow me to continue, as he was afraid for me. We had all been quite determined to do it this time because we'd had to postpone time and time again because of bad weather; I nevertheless made £800 – a lot of money in those days. I have always enjoyed swimming; even though I'm in my eighties I still swim in the open-air pool – and afterwards I rush home on my bike and dive into a hot bath!

Elsa Bulmer

Elsa Bulmer during her brave swim across the Solent.

Petersfield Music Festival

When I was at the Petersfield High School we used to enter a choir for the Petersfield Music Festival and I was a member from 1938. The Festival Hall had been built by that time (first used in 1936) and many high-powered people came, including Sir Adrian Boult, Sir Malcolm Sargent, Herbert Howells and Ralph Vaughan Williams. During the war, we held the festival in July so that we could have the concerts in the early evening and people would still be able to get home before dark; we didn't always have the staging up because the Festival Hall was also the main ARP base. After we were married, Alan joined the festival choir, which met on Monday nights, and I joined the Thursday singers – that way we could cover the babysitting. Alan was a Welshman and had a good voice; he was Chairman of Youth Day during the 1960s and '70's and he eventually became President of the Music Festival. I got back into the festival choir by about 1960 and I have sung most years ever since.

Mary Ray

Festival choirs

In 1948, after a Saturday afternoon concert by the Petersfield Orchestra, Sir Adrian Boult unveiled the Flora Twort portrait of Dr Harry Roberts. We youngsters were roped in to act as ushers. Doctor Harry Roberts lived locally but had a practice in the East End and that must indicate that he had a social conscience. He obviously became interested in the musical festival and spearheaded the drive to raise £5,000 to build what is now known as the Festival Hall. Lord Horder, the King's physician (who lived at Ashford Chase) and Dr Roberts wrote several theological books between them. All the big houses round Petersfield had servants and they would choose their new staff at the Michaelmas hiring fair.

Prior to being hired, each prospective employee was asked if they sang soprano, alto, tenor or base – because each house used to send their own choirs down to the festival!

Ken Hick

Singing in Hebrew

I started singing alto in the choir with my husband, Harry, when Sir Adrian Boult was conducting. In those days we had competitions; we got to the Town Hall at 9.00 a.m. and each individual choir sang for the silver cups and banners. In the afternoon we had to go back and rehearse for the evening performance. I gave it up when I had to sing in Hebrew – I managed the Latin but Hebrew was hopeless!

Nancy de Combe

Large Hall

The Festival Hall was initially known simply as the Large Hall because it had never been given a name. It was named after the 1979 improvements, so it must have been around 1982 that it first became known as the Festival Hall, commemorating the Petersfield Music Festival, which was founded in 1901. The Large Hall was built on the back of the Town Hall in 1935 and was opened on 6 October 1936 – Taro Fair Day – the money having been raised by the Music Festival. The festival used to be held in a building on the east side of Dragon Street; it is now called The Maltings but originally it was known as the Drill Hall – the only big venue in Petersfield at the time. The Corn Exchange, which was built in 1866, was converted for retail use in 1928, so it couldn't have been held there and I have never seen record of it being held anywhere but the Drill Hall.

Ken Hick

Flanders & Swann

The Flanders & Swann performances all happened by accident. I am Flanders, and William Godfree, director of music at Highfield, the Liphook preparatory school, is Swann. Our children were there together and I got to know William and liked him. He puts on a concert every summer called 'Music for a Summer Evening' and one day we agreed to play a piano duet – Ravel's *Mother Goose* – it went down rather well and we enjoyed doing it. Later, there was a concert in Farnham Castle and we were asked if we would do it again. We went to the rehearsal and it was so heavy that the person running it said, 'Is there anything you can do to lighten it up?' I asked William if he knew any Flanders and Swann songs and he said, 'Can a duck swim?' We did the 'Transport of Delight' (the one about the bus), and 'Mud, Mud, Glorious Mud'; it went down an absolute ball and someone said, 'You should do the whole thing.' This had never occurred to us but we thought, well why not! The very first one we did was for Naomi House, the Children's Hospice in Winchester. I went to what was then Southern Television and asked them to sponsor us and they agreed. We then went to Winchester College and they agreed have us in the hall and put up a marquee in the Provost's garden. We raised £11-12,000. That is how it was all born. The next big one was in the Redgrave Theatre in Farnham for the Leonard Cheshire Home at Le Court and that performance raised £8-9,000. We have done it in Petersfield for Vision Aid, in Steep for the village hall, and many others. We have almost exhausted the audience down here but people come to see it again and again and we have recently added new material from other composers of similar songs; we enjoy doing it and it's all in a good cause. We've been doing it in different parts of the country some three or four times a year for the past seven or eight

Michael Mates (standing) and William Godfree as Flanders & Swann, photographed at Churcher's College in 2003.

years and have raised over £120,000 for national and local charities.

Michael Mates, MP

Pop-in Club

When I retired I worked in the Petersfield Pop-in Club for ten years, making teas and looking after the customers. Everybody was welcome, whether they were lonely or if they were simply waiting for a bus. Village buses would only go about twice a day so once you had done your shopping you needed somewhere to wait. It's still offering the same service to this day.

Phyllis Gilburd

Operatic Society and Gilbert & Sullivan Society

The wonderful theatrical experiences at Churcher's College led me to being a stagehand for the 1951 Gilbert & Sullivan Society performance of *The Gondoliers* in the Town Hall and then actually joining the chorus in 1952 when they performed *The Mikado*. That was the last one produced by Basil Jimson, a Bedales teacher whose father had been part of the Arts and Crafts Movement with Edward Barnsley in Froxfield. Edward Barnsley also used to perform in the Operatic Society as a tenor lead. It was founded in 1922 and performed in the old Corn Exchange but in 1928 that was converted to retail use so the society didn't have a home; they then moved to the large hall at the Town Hall in 1936. They were going to stage *Iolanthe* in December 1939 but of course it was curtailed because of the war but, when the Operatic Society started again in 1950, they opened with *Iolanthe*. I am tempted to say it goes from strength to strength but we have suffered a big loss in Michael Harding's recent death; Michael produced us since about 1968. I had

Wartime production of The Mikado.

Wartime production of The Pirates of Penzance.

two years in the RAF – two 'wasted' years I wouldn't have missed for anything – and then in November 1989 I was due to play a part in *Sorcerer* when, a week before the show, I was taken off to hospital with pancreatitis. I have missed just three productions since I was a boy.

Ken Hick

Fashion icon

I designed and made all my own clothes and was very interested in fashion. My father, Harold Danby, was a carpenter for Mr Holder, the Petersfield builder, and he used to help me make clothes because he could measure accurately. Shorts were considered very daring in those days and one day the butcher was quite shocked when I wore a sleeveless dress! During the war I made coats out of blankets and we used to melt old gramophone records in hot water and make jewellery; it was pretty ghastly but it used to do!

Phyllis Gilburd

Cricket

After the war I took up cricket. My friend, Joyce Knowles, played for the Civil Service as an opening bowler and an opening bat and together we started the Post Office Telephones team. I was the wicket keeper. For a short while I also belonged to the Farnham Ladies' cricket team. I should have started years before but my parents didn't approve.

Margaret Childs

Badminton

The Bonham-Carters built the village hall for Sheet as part of their largesse. Outside there

Phyllis and Norman Gilburd in 1934.

are buttresses holding the walls up and if you go inside you will see there are metal ties that go up to the ridge. Bonham-Carter had discovered this new game that had been brought over from the North American Indians called 'badminton' and they decided they would like to play in the hall they had given to the village. They needed extra height so they cut the ties and put them up to the ridge. Unfortunately, the walls started to settle outwards so that is why they had to add the buttresses, to hold the walls up!

Ken Hick

Telephone exchange cricket team. Margaret Childs is between the bats, and captain Joyce Knowles is on her right.

The Harting cricket team, c. 1940. Roy Sherrington is in the second row, third from left; Bill Sherrington is in the bottom row, second from left. Mr Greetham was the umpire and a teacher at Liss School.

Bird nesting

Giggy and I went bird nesting – although we didn't reckon to take all the eggs from the nest. We liked collecting moorhen eggs, which we took home and cooked for tea. We also had our special 'withy' trees for collecting good stout sticks for bow shafts and arrows. One day, when we were up a tree busy cutting sticks for our bows, I said to Giggy, 'I've got a good one,' and a hand grabbed my leg and a voice said, 'So have I!' – it was Mr Rice, the Smart's farm foreman! He frightened the life out of us; always after that it was 'Look out! here comes old tapioca!'

Heath House (which in my young days belonged to a Miss Runell, but when Mum was young belonged to the lord of the manor, Lord Hylton) was where Mum used to work with her mother in the kitchen. Giggy and I used to climb the big fir trees that surrounded the house to collect rooks eggs. One March, I had climbed this big tree of about fifty feet and was amongst these huge rooks nests, trying to avoid being dive-bombed by the very upset rooks, when all of a sudden it started to blow hard and rain. I was terrified so I just clung on to the main trunk for what seemed hours; eventually I did manage to get down to earth, wet through with a pocket full of crushed rooks eggs – Mum wasn't too pleased about that.

On a fine Sunday Giggy and I would go off for a long tramp over the hills; we would take some bread and a bottle of water, then if we were lucky enough to find a pheasant's nest, we would light a small fire and boil the eggs in a small tin which we had taken with us. They were delicious.

Harry Edwards

Cinema

On Wednesdays we would spend threepence and go to the local cinema but eventually the staff got to know me and they used to let me in for nothing. Sometimes we would be given an orange or a picture of Tom Mix, the well-known cowboy (or whoever was the star of the film that week). The music was live and was chosen according to whether it was exciting or sad. They had serials where they would show you a bit, and then right at the high spot they'd say, 'come next week' – that was as well as the big picture. My brother Bert worked at the Home & Colonial Grocery Store, not far from the cinema, and when they closed on Fridays he used to bring left-over lemon cake; it was beautiful when it was fresh but it would go dry very quickly.

Earnest Foard

Silent films

It was all silent films: *Dan Dare*, *Fatty Arbuckle* and *Buster Keeton* were our favourites. Mrs Le Goubin used to play the piano down in the pit in front of the screen and if there were horses on the film she would bang two halves of a coconut shell together and if it was a rough sea, pieces of sandpaper would be rubbed together. We all used to cheer Mrs Le Goubin for her piano playing, although what she played didn't matter two hoots to us. It amused us when the sequences of the film changed and we were getting sea sounds for galloping horses; the poor woman couldn't get changed over quick enough, but we didn't mind! The figures on the film were sort of jerky and they appeared to be doing about twenty miles per hour and the horses, well, I don't know what speed they did! During the interval Mr Lemon, the manager, would come around with a spray that was like one of those old-fashioned fly sprayers, and he would pump this scented spray up and down the gangways – whether it was because we 'ponged' or it was something to do with regulations, I wouldn't know! The noise of all the children was deafening and, sitting on hard, tip-up seats, we soon got restless.

Harry Edwards

Playtime

We didn't have a lot, so we used to make our own pleasures. One day a lady came to the door and said that her son had outgrown his toys. She gave me a box of toys but then said, 'I have a scooter and a bicycle and you can choose which one you would like.' I chose the scooter and I used to go up, as well as down, Bell Hill; I became quite an expert on it. We also had iron wheels as hoops with a metal 'teeler', like a piece of bent wire which you would put on the wheel and then you would run with it – you could get up some terrific speeds with it. The ladies had wooden hoops that they used with the hand. We used to like standing on the walkway over the railway when the steam engines went under us; the steam had a lovely smell.

Earnest Foard

Mud larks

We used to cycle to Horndean, leave our bikes at the pub then get onto the tram to

Portsmouth, which cost about 9d each return. We would go around the shops in Portsmouth or go down to Southsea beach; we used to like to see the boys diving in the mud down by the dockyard. They'd ask you to throw pennies and would dive for them in the slimy mud, and they were known as 'mud larks'. We would have a nice day sightseeing and then take our tram back to Horndean where we would collect our bikes. During the whole seven-mile ride you might have seen a farm cart or a brewer's dray with horses or a couple of cyclists, but usually you would just see hundreds of wild rabbits and sheep grazing on the Downs. There were also no trees, only the old yew tree that had been there for hundreds of years.

Harry Edwards

Sheet Mill

A great friend of mine was a chap called Les Nation and he told me once that they'd dammed the river, upstream of the old Sheet Mill. They had some changing cubicles and we used to pay 1s 6d a month to swim there. Nobody seems to know anything about that so perhaps it only operated for a couple of years. It was said that someone drowned there.

Ken Hick

Hayling Billy

I used to go to Sunday school and then we'd all trot off to church, but I'm afraid several of us became absent at the church door as there were quite a lot of big tombstones in the churchyard which were good hiding places! However, we still managed to get a ticket for the annual church outing to Hayling Island, sometime in June. We would all meet at the school at about 8.30 a.m. and then march to

Petersfield station; we would pile into a carriage, at least a dozen in each compartment – in those days all compartments were separate. Including teachers and perhaps some parents there would be about 100 of us. When we reached Havant, our coaches would be taken off the Portsmouth train and little *Hayling Puffing Billy* would be coupled on – and off we'd go to Hayling Island. On arrival we had to walk a mile to the beach but on getting there it was wonderful. We spent the whole day in the sea or building sandcastles. At 5.00 p.m. we were rounded up and marched to the Victoria Hall where a good tea was ready for us. Then we had about an hour's 'magic lantern show' – that's a sort of lamp in which they inserted slides with people or scenery on them and this was projected onto a white screen – we thought it was marvellous. Then it was the journey home by train with all of us singing and happy as sand boys.

Harry Edwards

Skating

1926 was a terrible winter and we had lots of snow. The stable boys had to dig a trench through the snow from where we lived to the bottom of the Causeway; it was at least four feet high because I couldn't see over the top and there was just enough room for us to walk down. I had skates screwed onto the bottom of my riding boots and went skating on the Heath Lake; before we could skate properly we used to tie cushions onto ourselves! I used to stand for hours and watch old Mrs Reeves skating; she had some high lace-up boots and she used to put her hands in a muff – she skated marvellously!

Nancy Ford

Above: *The Harting Football Club, c. 1926. Reg Sherrington is on the left in the front row; Bill Sherrington is in the second row on the right.*

Opposite: *Skating on Petersfield Heath in 1937. Sam Hardy can be seen with pipe and Pansy Bonham-Carter is on his left.*

Frozen

I did a lot of roller skating when I was young and I often ice skated on the Petersfield Lake when it froze over. I skated on ice skates from Sheet to Petersfield one winter – I think it was 1938 or '39; we had what was called an ice storm and all the hedges and the little twigs were thick with ice and the branches were falling off.

Norman Gilburd

8 Famous Faces

Flora Twort

I used to know the artist Flora Twort very well. She used to come into my shop and buy all her fruit and have long chats. She sometimes lent us the mill she owned at Langstone and we used to go down there and stay the weekend. Flora had the shop next to Baileys where she used to sell lovely jewellery, curios, books and, of course, her pictures. She was a bit quaint and rather reserved. She never married.

Nancy de Combe

A lovely lady

I got to know the artist Flora Twort through a shared desire to see a community centre in Petersfield. She was a lovely lady. Flora was the Lowry of this part of the country; she recorded Petersfield as it was at a time when it was all going to change.

Ken Hick

Flora drew me

I remember, as a little girl, going round to the shop at No. 1 The Square where Flora Twort, Miss Brahms and Miss Wagstaff worked. I used to sit by their fire and talk to all the ladies. Flora drew me when I was about six years old; I think she did my brother and sister but I have lost those pictures. My family used to cut her

hair; she was quite a weird lady, very Bohemian, and always had very straight hair and a fringe. She painted the views of the market from her window, all of which are well known. She did two lovely paintings called *Ten-to-nine* and *Ten-past-twelve*, of children going to and from school and I'm sure they were done from that window.

Margaret Maybrey

Twickenham streaker

Erika Roe worked for me for about two years. The first I knew of her topless streak at Twickenham during the England Rugby International was when the *News of the World* came round to interview me! She put the shop and Petersfield on the map! I was booking into a hotel in San Francisco and they saw 'Petersfield' and they said, 'Oh, do you know the Petersfield bookshop?' The last I heard was that she was living in Portugal.

Our son John travels all over the country to buy book collections or private libraries but he is famous for being a big fan of Portsmouth Football Club and for changing his name to John Portsmouth Football Club Westwood.

Frank Westwood

Royal 'Navvy'

Princess Margaret's two children went to Bedales. The boy hadn't been there many

The late Flora Twort, centre, with Ann and Frank Westwood of the Petersfield bookshop.

weeks and one day I saw them giving him a rough time – throwing turfs at him – but he settled in very well I think. I once had some brick rubble in a bucket so I said, 'Hold that for me David', so he held it for a while and then said, 'What shall I do with it?' I said 'Take it down the stairs and tip it out,' so he did – so I can say I once had royal people working for me! A lot of famous actors' children also went to Bedales.

Norman Gilburd

Norman Hartnell

Mother was the Lady Patroness of the hunt ball and Norman Hartnell had just started work and he made a dress for her for five guineas.

Charles Hardy

Craftsmen

We have had a number of gifted craftsmen in Petersfield: George Taylor, a furniture maker *par excellence* has won the prize for wildlife carving for several years (he carves our names on the board of honour in the council chamber); Bert Upton who worked for Edward Barnsley; Harold Thompson who was one of the thirty top stained-glass window artists in the country, and of course Edward Barnsley, furniture maker. John Barnsley, son of Edward Barnsley, is still producing wonderful furniture; I suppose their pride and joy is a rosewood board table they made for Cortaulds. Arthur Negus was once asked 'If you were to buy something today to hand down to your family as an heirloom, what would you buy?' He replied, 'A bit of Edward Barnsley furniture'.

Ken Hick

Famous ancestors

My mother and her twin sister were famous in Australia. Their great, great grandfather was Admiral Philip Gidley King who went out with the first fleet and was the third governor of New South Wales in 1800; his daughter married Hannibal Hawkins Macarthur, the nephew of John Macarthur, whose profile was on the 1980s Australian two dollar bill. My father is descended from Thomas Masterman Hardy who attended Nelson during his dying moments and who went on to become the first Sea Lord in 1830. We think there is a family connection with Thomas Hardy, the novelist and poet, but we haven't been able to prove it conclusively.

Charles Hardy

Charles Hardy, 2003.

Are you being served?

E.J. Baker was a butcher and he had his own abattoir at the Grange. His son was the actor who starred as Brough, the old boy in the television programme *Are you being served?*

Norman Bryant

Wedgwood

I looked after Lady Wedgwood's mother up at Shear Hill. Lord Wedgwood was only forty when he died. That was one of the saddest days of my life – he was such a nice man.

June Walker

Sir Alec and Lady Guinness

Sir Alec Guinness lived in Steep until he died and I used to see him at the Garrick Club in London. He was the most charming, unassuming and terribly nice man. He once said, 'Well done, you haven't upset my wife lately,' so I said, 'I'm very pleased about that!' She was a rabid Liberal and the very first time I was canvassing I knocked on her door (he obviously wasn't there and I didn't know who she was) and she said, 'Please don't call on this house again, we are not Conservatives.' I said, 'Fine, I have just called to say hello.' I mentioned it to Sir Alec and said, 'I got the bum's rush at your house,' and he said, 'Yes, you would!'

Michael Mates MP

Expensive strawberries

One day I had a few out-of-season strawberries for sale but they were terrifically expensive. There was a little lady with freckles standing in the queue at the shop and she said, 'May I have six boxes of strawberries please?' I said, 'I'm afraid they are very expensive.' She

Charles Hardy, age four, with his mother (right) and aunt – the Macarthur twins.

looked at me very disdainfully and said, 'I asked for six boxes of strawberries', so I wrapped them up for her. The lady next to me said, 'You know who you have just been arguing with, don't you – it was only Lady Guinness!' I went on to give her stuff for her goats.

Norman Bryant

The 'gardener'

When Sir Alec Guinness and his wife Merula moved into Kettlebrook Meadows in Steep, they naturally came to the best shop in Petersfield for their house furnishings. Dad went up to the house to talk to Mrs Guinness (as she was then) about what she wanted. He walked into the garden and there was this chap who he took to be the gardener. He asked if Mrs Guinness was in and he said that she was

up in the house. Dad wandered up the garden and this chap followed him and hovered in the background while Dad talked to Mrs Guinness. Off Dad went to do the estimates, and the next day this smartly dressed gentleman came into the shop and said, 'You were up at my house yesterday...' the 'gardener' was Alec Guinness who had just finished making the film *The Prisoner*! Dad said that he was frantically trying to remember if he had said anything wrong but Sir Alec was always was a very modest gentleman – in the true sense of the word. We finished the job successfully but, about six or eight weeks later, we had to do the curtains all over again – they had a parrot that had gone berserk and ripped the curtains to shreds!

Mary Vincent

The King and Wallis

My father's best man and his wife were called Mr and Mrs George Hunter (they were also my godparents) and they were friendly with the Americans, Mr and Mrs Earnest Simpson. The Hunter's brought the Simpsons to Petersfield and they all went to Goodwood together. One day, my godfather rang my father and said, 'In order to get her divorce Wallis has to stay at a house in Felixstowe and the King wants Kitty and I to go and stay with her because nobody else seems to be going there.' After a few days my godfather rang again and said, 'Sam, can you come up to Felixstowe because there's only Wallis, Kitty and myself and we want another for a hand of bridge – we're all bored to tears!' By then my father didn't much approve of what was going on between Wallis and the King but he was quite truthful when he said, 'I'm sorry George, I don't play bridge' – but he wouldn't have gone anyway and he refused to have Wallis here without Earnest. However, I have a signed card responding to my letter of

Sam Hardy with his beloved dog Tess in 1912.

condolence on the death of the Duke of Windsor which was sent by Wallis, and inscribed on the back are the words, 'Will never forget Sam's kindness to us,' so perhaps father relented in the end?

My godfather used to get very fed up with all the awful things they used to write about the Duke of Windsor and he would tell us many stories of the Duke's sense of humour, kindness and generosity, especially when my godparents were a bit short of money. 'How are you off for l.s.d. [money], could you do with a couple of thousand?' the Duke would ask. George would demur and the King would say, 'I'll put a cheque in the post.'

Charles Hardy

Royal visitors

The Queen came in her Silver Jubilee year to open the Queen Elizabeth Country Park and that was when Lord Porchester was the Chairman of the Hampshire County Council.

We had lunch afterwards and I was sitting next to her. I said, 'You may be interested to know that the wine you are drinking is grown in the constituency, about five miles away.' We had given her some of the Hambledon white wine. She said, 'Oh, that's dear Guido.' Well, that was Major General Sir Guy Salisbury-Jones to me! He had been the Marshal of the Diplomatic Corps, so obviously they knew each other terribly well. He had retired to Hambledon and set up the vineyard. She then said, 'He sent me a case of their first vintage'. When I next went to see him, I went into his downstairs loo and there was a framed hand-written letter saying, 'Dear Guido, thank you so much for the wine, I do congratulate you on your achievement, Yours, Elizabeth.'

We've had lots of royal visitors over the years: the Duchess of Gloucester came to open Gloucester Court and, in May 1990, the Physic Garden. We've had Prince Phillip at HMS *Mercury* and RAF Oakhanger. The Prince of Wales came to Durford Mill about three or four years ago to visit a high-tech sound system company there – I used to live at Durford Mill House so he was a few yards from my home! I think Princess Anne has been down to the horse trials at Stocklands, near Liphook and, of course, Princess Alexandra lit the beacon for the Silver Jubilee celebrations – when I last met her she reminisced about the occasion.

Michael Mates MP

Queen Alexandra

When my father was at school at Harrow, Queen Alexandra came to visit. He was running the band and the Queen stopped and asked them to play a particular tune. This upset all the plans but she wanted to listen to the music. She thanked him and from that day on he sent her birthday congratulations on the 1 December – and raised the Union Jack at the top of Hardy House in The Spain. She replied with signed photographs. The odd thing is that on the day she died in 1925 there was a storm, and lightening struck his flagpole and it fell to the ground. The man who later did the work on the flagpole told me that he'd offered to repair it immediately but my father said, 'No, the Queen's dead so I won't be flying it any more.' I was born the following year, on the 1 December 1926, the late Queen's birthday. My father rang him at five o'clock in the morning telling him to 'put that flagpole right at once.' Then the flag was raised to announce my birth.

Charles Hardy

Godfrey Evans

Grandfather Tubbs used to go up to the Jolly Drover to pay his club dues and he knew Godfrey Evans, the cricketer, who was the landlord then.

Jennifer Robinson

Admirals and Generals

I knew Admiral Sir Michael Le Fanu, the First Lord of the Admiralty, very well. He often used to come to the Drum and we'd have a drink together. Shortly after the day he was made First Sea Lord he stood outside the shop looking for me and said, 'Do you fancy a drink Norman?' and I said, 'Yes, but I don't know what to say on this great occasion. I've never congratulated anybody on this sort of promotion.' And he said to me, 'Do you know Norman, of all the congratulations I've had I think yours is the nicest of the lot.' Before he was made up he went to America as one of the leading lights of the English Navy; I was serving on the stall and two smart gentlemen were standing there, all gold braid and medals – I thought they were customs officers! I asked if I could help them and they said, 'Yes, we have come to the Naval Barracks at Leydene and we have been commanded by Captain Le Fanu to look for a Norman Bryant and buy him a drink.' Commanded!

Norman Bryant

Field Marshals

There have been all sorts of famous military people in the constituency. When I first came here there were at least five Field Marshal equivalents: there was Field Marshal Sir 'Roly' Gibbs, Field Marshal Lord Carver, Admiral of the Fleet Sir Edward Ashmore, Field Marshal Lord Bramall and Admiral Sir David Williams.

Michael Mates MP

Pickwick gentleman

Sam Hardy was the lord mayor of Petersfield, the Squire, but he was a real 'Pickwick'

Homeward bound! Sam Hardy driving up Sheep Street in 1921.

gentleman. We had a milk round as well as the farm and he was our best customer, but he never had no money. He once owed us quite a lot – about £90, which before the war was a lot of money. At an appropriate moment I said to Sam, 'My father is worried about your bill, Sir.' He said, 'Oh, why didn't you mention it before? I'll give you my mother's address up in Northumberland and all you've got to do is write to her and tell her that her Sam owes £90 and she'll send the money.' And she did! Thereafter, as soon as we thought the bill had got a bit high, we wrote to his mother! By then he was going a little bit broke. He could spend a fortune without women, gambling or drink; he had all these horses and carriages and he would buy farms and almost give them away. He was a very generous man. I was very upset when he died. He even came to my twenty-first birthday all dressed up in his Scottish kilt and sang his Harry Lauder songs.

Norman Bryant

Dan Pearson

I had no children of my own but I became friendly with Daniel and Luke Pearson, two young neighbours who lived with their artistic parents, Sheila and Ray. Our friendship began when Dan and Luke tried to make a pond in my garden, and Dan became very interested in plants. He was only about seven or eight when he began entering competitions in the local gardening club. He wasn't very interested in schoolwork in those days – gardening was his first love; but how he has changed – his books, television programmes and articles for the *Sunday Times* are superb. He had a very good English teacher (Mrs Wiggins) at Midhurst Middle School and she helped him a great deal. The people at Greatham Mill greatly inspired him, but he always said I was his guru! I remember when he had a stall at the end of the lane and he would sell plants he had propagated himself. Even when he became famous he continued to help me in my garden

Left: *Geraldine Noyes, 2003.*

Above: *Daniel Pearson, celebrity gardener.*

when he came home for the weekend. His knowledge of plants is phenomenal, most of it self-taught before he got a scholarship to Wisley and Kew. It was exciting when Daniel started putting things into Chelsea; I was once in hospital in Southampton but despite the fact that he was working towards Chelsea, he still came down to see me – with a huge bouquet of flowers.

Geraldine Noyes

Lillie Langtry and Vesta Tilley

In the 1920s Harry Lauder was staying with my father in The Spain. Also staying in the neighbourhood was the actress Lillie Langtry (then Lady de Bathe, wife of Sir Hugo de Bathe) and the music hall star Vesta Tilley (then Lady de Frece, wife of Sir Walter de Frece). Sir Harry said, 'Let's have the de Bathes and the de Freces over to dinner.' However, he admitted, 'I've done it for fun,

Sam, because they are like a couple of Kilkenny cats – they hate each other and have been hating each other since 1870!' They sat down to dinner and father said it was, 'Could you pass the salt, Lady de Bathe,' and, 'certainly, Lady de Frece,' and eventually Harry Lauder banged the table and said, 'We've had enough of this, I'm sick of this Lady de Bathe-ing and this Lady de Frece-ing – you're Lillie and she's Vesta and that's it!'

Charles Hardy

Queen Mary

When Queen Mary came to Uppark we all had to go outside and curtsy to her. She was very nice though and she spoke to each of us. I had to curtsy and I nearly fell over! Of course, in the Victorian days, the mother of H.G. Wells was the housekeeper.

Violet Sherrington

111

Charles Seaward OBE and his wife May in 1939.

Charles and May Seaward

When Charles Seaward received his OBE from the King in about 1935 he told my father that he didn't know what to say to the King so he said, in his real Hampshire voice, 'Wonderful day for 'aying, Your Majesty.' They were a wonderful couple and everyone loved them. They married in 1902 and their honeymoon was two nights in the Ship Hotel in Brighton, then they came back to Borough House and never spent another night away from Petersfield for the rest of their lives. It wasn't anything to do with money because they were very well off. He died in 1955 and she died ten days later; they never quite knew why she died because the doctor said there was nothing wrong with Aunt May. Uncle Charlie was laid out in their very ornate dining room and her maid, Alice, heard old Mrs Seaward go in, give her husband a kiss on the head and say, 'I won't be long dear,' and within ten days she was gone. They say it must have been from a broken heart.

Charles Hardy

Gunning King and Tommy Cooper

We often had the well-known Harting artist Gunning King in the shop. Mr King was a frequent exhibitor at the Royal Academy and was awarded a gold medal at the International Exhibition at the Crystal Palace in 1899. One day he did a cartoon of my grandfather and father, which was published in *Punch*. Grandfather is seen receiving some money from a customer before a haircut and the customer is saying, 'This is not a tip this is 'hush' money' – which meant keep quiet while you are doing my hair! They were pretty good likenesses. Tommy Cooper came in for a haircut once; he was just the same as on television.

John Freeman

Beautiful hands

My father posed as Jesus Christ for Gunning King's painting *Christ and the Fishermen*, now

Gunning King's 1919 cartoon of the Freemans.

Margaret Maybrey (née Lee), poses in front of the Gunning King painting for which her father, Bill Lee, posed as Christ.

hanging in the chancel of St Peter's church. Mr King said father had beautiful hands. At one time you could see the painting from the pews and my mother used to love sitting in church, looking up into the face of her husband.

Margaret Maybrey

Ruth Rendell and Pamela Stevenson

One of the Ruth Rendell television series, *Road Rage*, was filmed in Petersfield and they used the children's library – that was an interesting day. We had Pamela Stevenson's bed in the library window once: it had been made for her and so it was displayed before she took delivery of it.

Des Farnham

Silver Jubilee

As a young reporter on the *Petersfield Herald* I had many memorable assignments, but the 1977 Queen Elizabeth Silver Jubilee celebrations must surely be paramount. I represented the newspaper on Butser Hill when Princess Alexandra, accompanied by her husband Mr Angus Ogilvie and children Marina and James, lit the Silver Jubilee beacon. What my editor didn't know is that I almost missed it! I was stuck in a traffic jam on the A3 but fortunately my family was with me and my husband was driving so, in true hack spirit, I jumped out of the car and ran up the south side of Butser Hill. I arrived very red faced and feeling sick but made it ahead of the Royal entourage – just! I then spent a pleasant evening in royal company with Mr Ogilvie informally telling me that, having been press ganged into taking the salute at some of the smaller parades, he felt decidedly awkward. 'I don't even have a Scouts uniform to wear' he said, 'and I didn't know what to do with my hands when they saluted me.'

Pamela Payne

9 Politics, Law and Order

Our Member of Parliament

I was a career army officer and had no experience of politics but I'd been interested in what was going on and I'd had two very political jobs that brought me into the front line. The first was in Northern Ireland in 1969 and then in 1973 I was in the Ministry of Defence working for the Chief of the Defence Staff on terrorism, which was a pretty new and political subject. I got interested and thought that it was no use just complaining about the socialist determination to cut our defence budget, I must get involved. I applied but never expected to get accepted. There was a very fraught time, after the miner's strike and the three-day week, when Harold Wilson won the February 1974 election by three or four votes, and my predecessor, Joan Quennell, resigned very suddenly and unexpectedly in July of that year. The Liberals were making a big attempt to take the seat and they took her majority down from 20,000 to 7,000; I think she thought the skids were under her and that everyone was disillusioned with politics so she left. All the candidates on the shortlist had been politicians and three of them subsequently made the Cabinet but I was a fresh face and an outsider and I think they thought they should try something new. I got selected on the 22 August, left the Army on 1 September and went into the House on 11 October 1974, which was all pretty fast. We lived in Petersfield for ten years but now live just 500 yards over the Hampshire border in West Sussex. I have always found Petersfield to be a thoroughly nice, civilised, friendly town with everything going for it and lots of lovely people working for the good of the community.

Michael Mates MP

Little wonder!

The electorate of Petersfield (now East Hants) has, with just one exception (1866-1885), always returned a Conservative since elections began in the eighteenth century. But in the 1930s, my father and Charlie Seaward (Chairman of the Petersfield Conservative Party for about fifty years) were famous for things they shouldn't have done, politically! The limekilns at Butser employed a lot of men and Dad told me that they knew all these people would vote Labour. The 'Little Wonder' bus went to and from Butser, so on Election Day they made sure it was 'broken' and didn't run; by the time they'd all walked to Petersfield, the polls were closed!

Charles Hardy

Prime Minister

Not many people know that we've even had a Prime Minister as Member of Parliament for Petersfield: George Canning was a Tory Prime Minister for just four months during 1827. He entered Parliament in 1793, fought a duel

Michael Mates MP, 2003.

with the War Minister, Viscount Castlereagh, formed a coalition with the Whigs and died in office in 1827. His son, Charles, first Earl Canning, was the first viceroy of India from 1858.

Michael Mates MP

Out of the Blue concert party

I was Vice Chairman of the Young Conservatives from 1950 to 1952 and I went to those big rallies in the Albert Hall several times and met Winston Churchill and Anthony Eden. Mrs Garner, of Gammon & Garner, the coal people, ran an 'Out of the Blue' concert party; we used to take my piano and go all round the village halls once or twice a week. Reeves Removals would move the piano and we also had their lorry when we did open house speaking in The Square, when people would argue politics in the open air.

Nancy de Combe

Four MPs

There have been only four members of Parliament since the war: General Sir George Jeffreys, 1941-1951; The Hon. Peter Legh (who became Lord Newton), 1951-1960; Miss Joan Quennell, 1960-1974; and myself. I am coming up to thirty years and, if the electorate don't retire me, I shall do one more. I have been Chairman of the Defence Committee and Minister of State in Northern Ireland, responsible for security. I now chair the Northern Ireland Committee and sit on the Prime Minister's Intelligence Committee.

Michael Mates MP

Marzipan hat

I was Mayor of Petersfield three times. Elsa Bulmer has just retired after thirty-five years as a councillor, so I am lagging behind – I have only done twenty-nine years! I had a break for nine years simply because of work commitments.

I always refer to the loos in the central car park as Elsa's loos because they were her idea. Shortly after the town council was founded we had an amusing situation when Elsa said she would eat her hat if it happened. Well it did happen and we had to solve the problem of Elsa eating her hat, so I had a little marzipan hat made for her; she never did eat it but kept it in a showcase until it eventually fell to bits!

Ken Hick

Penns Place

At least eight generations of the Penn family have been born in Sheet since the 1570s. Penn is a famous name in Petersfield, i.e. Penns Place where the East Hants District Council offices now stand. The first known record of the Penn family in Petersfield is 1265 when

Out of the Blue concert party, held around 1950.

Conservative dance at Drill Hall, Dragon Street, in 1926.

Elsa Bulmer on her retirement after thirty-five years in local government. Courtesy of Petersfield Post.

the land was gifted to a William de Penn who farmed the land that became known as Penn's Farm. The records are not very clear from the 1500s and we are not terribly sure of the connection thereafter but, nevertheless, the East Hants District Council discussed the naming of the county council offices with my family before deciding upon Penns Place.

Clinton Brown

Urban District Council

When I first became a Member of Parliament, the East Hants District Council was brand new and had only just had its first elections. It had changed from being the Petersfield Urban District Council and the EHDC was finding its way. People hate change you know; everybody is conservative with a small 'c'; they like things as they are.

Michael Mates MP

Town and district

One of the great assets of the Petersfield Urban District Council, as opposed to the EHDC, was that we had no politics. With one exception, I had no idea what the political allegiances were of any of my colleagues; we were just a council helping the Petersfield people. We looked after everything from planning to public health (we even had a morgue with Dr Farr in charge) and we also built three very large social housing estates. What was so important was that we got down to everything; we didn't have to keep having resolutions, whereas now, as a town council, we have our difficulties because some of our twelve town councillors are also on the East Hants District Council, so there is conflict between town and district. The days of the Urban District Council were halcyon days when much was achieved.

Elsa Bulmer

Rommel

I went onto the Urban District Council in 1965 when there were no political parties involved or the need to separate party political from political. We ran the market, the minor roads and the sewage works; we'd just given up the waterworks to make sure that water provision was standard, and we also inspected meat at the abattoir; we had a Medical Officer of Health, Alan Farr, who we shared with the rural district council (he had had experience out in Africa as a professional Medical Officer of Health). John Thomas, the Borough Engineer, was a very capable man who, when he was a prisoner of war, had spoken to Rommel. He was a water engineer and was therefore asked to represent the prisoners of war and to ask Rommel for a special water ration – Rommel told him in no uncertain terms that they didn't get any less than his own

Above: *The final meeting of the Petersfield Urban District Council, in 1974.*

Right: *Ken Hick.*

troops! The Building Control Inspector, a Mr Watts, was a bit of a 'shadowy' (not shady!) figure and he vanished under strange circumstances.

Ken Hick

Casting vote

It was a great honour to be made Chairman of the EHDC because I was one of only two Independents out of a total of thirty councillors: there were fifteen Liberals and thirteen combined Labour and Conservatives – and I suddenly realised I'd got the casting vote!

Elsa Bulmer

Council furniture

Dad made the Council Chamber furniture for the Petersfield Council when the Town Hall was built in 1936. It is still in use down at the District Council but they won't let us have it back! There wasn't any room for the furniture so it was put in store when the Urban District Council and the Rural District Council went to East Hampshire District Council. When the Petersfield Town Council asked for it back they said they knew nothing about it! That beautiful golden oak furniture is still as good as new.

Mary Vincent

The mace

In 1929 the Urban District Council petitioned the High Court to have the mace (inscribed March 23 1596, probably the oldest mace in the country) restored to the town of Petersfield from the Jolliffe family. I understand they had a stainless steel replica made of it before handing over the original to the council.

Ken Hick

Mary Vincent.

Honourable woman

My grandfather always said that he saw the bar as the means by which a young man of modest means could get into politics. When my grandfather became Lord Chancellor he had to take a peerage, so he became Viscount Simon and mother became an Honourable. This was really a big joke and our GP rang her up and said, 'Congratulations, I hear they've made an honourable woman of you at last – but there's no chance of you becoming a real lady, is there?' 'No,' she said, 'Thank goodness.'

Caroline Kennedy

Juvenile court

I was on the Bench for twenty-odd years and was chairman of the Juvenile court. When the youngsters were waiting to be seen by us they

Caroline Kennedy (Joan Bickford-Smith's daughter) in 2003.

were given a little tour of the cells, which did them the power of good! The schools would send their pupils to watch a court case and a couple of schoolteachers would be members of the Bench. Now, middle-aged men come up to me in the street and say 'I remember you, Mrs Bulmer, when you had me up in court. I am now happily married and I've got four kids!' Local firms would allow one of their staff to become a magistrate; this involved a lot of their employee's time but they thought they were doing a service to Petersfield and it all added up to a cohesion of a family.

Elsa Bulmer

Domestic violence

I was always very much aware that some women, victims of domestic violence, were alone and in distress in the middle of the night, without even a telephone number they could ring for help and advice. In the late 1980s the problem was being talked about, and friends of mine and other people I contacted set up an emergency phone line in a big wooden hut in my garden at Burnt Ash Cottages in Sheet. That offered at least a little help to 'battered wives' and allowed us to assess the extent of the need for a refuge in this part of East Hampshire. The women who came to staff the phone line decided to hold a public meeting in July 1990 at the Mill Chase Community School in Bordon. Lots of those who came shared their personal experiences with us that evening. We were very moved by their stories and felt their need for a refuge to be very urgent.

We managed to find a house in Liss but that only lasted about two or three years because one day a male window cleaner realised it was a refuge; he must have mentioned it to someone because before long there was an irate and vicious man at the door who had come to get his wife out. As a consequence, we had to immediately abandon the Liss house and find a new home. The East Hants District Council Housing Association was very good to us; they realised the dangers and they eventually found a suitable property in Alton. They furnished it with the basics and then we made an appeal for linen, curtains, cots, high chairs and so on; the local people were very generous. We have been in Alton ever since and the original warden is still there. It is beautifully decorated and comfortable and now it is going to be extended so that up to thirty-two women and children can be accommodated.

No one can say whether it is needed more now than before; there is more publicity about domestic violence today and the public is consequently made more aware of the problem. In the old days women just never admitted to it – it was almost a disgrace or a

The old courthouse (with waxwork judge!), now the Petersfield Museum. On the left are Mary Ray and Jill Thompson-Lewis. On the right is Doreen Binks.

failure on their part. The police were not involved with domestic problems, but of course they are now. As a result of our success, the police and social services now get phone calls from as far away as Portsmouth. They are all welcome and the one thing we do is to make them feel special because their self-esteem is absolutely broken.

Sheila Trueman and Elsa Bulmer

Patricide

Great-grandmother Rhoda had a sad life while she was married to great-grandfather Henry Knight. He had a terrible temper and would beat her but one day her son Jesse killed him while defending his mother. I'm glad to say he was acquitted.

Clinton Brown

Tramps

The tramps who appeared in court were mainly regulars attending for minor offences and we always paid their railway ticket out of Petersfield from the Poor Box. There was something of a rapport between us and they would address us as 'Sir' and 'Madam' – sometimes even 'Lord' and 'Lady'. However, on one occasion when we dismissed a case we were thanked profusely as 'Your Majesties'!

Elsa Bulmer

Hats off, lady magistrates

It was once *de rigueur* that all lady magistrates wore hats. My mother, Joan Bickford-Smith, told the story of her hat at her retirement gathering in 1973. 'You owe it to me that lady magistrates in Hampshire do not have to wear hats,' she said proudly. In 1940 the class structure was more rigid and the Chairman of the Bench was an elderly titled lady of whom my mother was very much in awe. On her first day, she sat on the Bench with this lady and, at the end of the day, Lady C said to her, 'And have you enjoyed it, my dear?' Ma said, 'Yes I have, but I don't think I can think all day in a hat.' Lady C replied, 'Well, don't wear one then.' My mother was so surprised; it was the last thing she expected her to say.

My mother told me that an old man of eighty-two was charged with driving without due care and attention. He brought his wife along with him as a witness because she was in the car when this incident occurred. My mother asked, 'And what gear were you in when you approached the junction?' and he said, 'You know, the usual gear.' When pressed he said, 'Top.' So then the old lady got into the witness box to give her account. She turned to my mother with a disarming smile and said, 'I am Dougie's eyes and ears when he is driving'! It was quite obvious that this old chap wasn't fit to be on the road because he was very nearly blind and deaf! So, they fined him for driving without due care and attention and mother said, very kindly, 'And we think that before you take your car out again you should have your sight and hearing tested, and you should take a driving test.' Well, that effectively got him off the road because he wasn't going to take a test at eighty-two, was he? In those days, people of that age would never have taken a test if they didn't let their license lapse.

Caroline Kennedy

Joan Bickford-Smith, 1946.

10 Taro Fair

Romany gypsies

We very much looked forward to the annual Taro Fair. I remember when they used to deal in horses. They had lovely roundabouts, swings, 'chairoplanes' and stalls. It was all run by several generations of Romany gypsies. The chap on the hammer that rings the bell was there every year from when he was a teenager; he is probably a pensioner now! Norman and I were married on 8 October 1936 on the day of the Taro Fair and all the gypsies stood outside to watch.

Phyllis Gilburd

Boxing ring

The boxing at the Taro Fair would be considered quite barbaric now. There was a professional boxer who would challenge anyone who would like to put on the gloves; they would pay prize money if you won but you'd have to be pretty good because the referee was always on the side of the fair man. We had some soldiers who boxed at Longmoor camp, and when they got into the ring the referee used to say, 'Take it a bit easy, mate, he's been boxing all evening and you've only got to go three rounds.' There was one fellow who boxed for the fair who became a professional; his name was Joe Beckett.

Norman Gilburd

Winkles for tea

The big occasion of the year was Taro Fair and we would troupe down there in our Sunday best. We only had buses from Buriton twice a week so we used to walk across the fields, through the bluebell woods and out into Sussex Road. Grandfather used to give me and my cousin, Eric Porter, half a crown for us to spend. When we got back to Sussex Road we'd have this wonderful tea but grandma used to have these cooked winkles, which I never liked because they smelled of vinegar – but she did make wonderful seed cake.

June Edwards

Wall of death

There was a dome of death with motor cycles going round that had to come right up to the top of this wall. Of course it was the speed that kept them on the wall but one year I saw them go right over the top! They always asked if anybody would like to have a try; well a lot of us were keen motor cyclists in those days so somebody went in to have a go and this fellow from the fair stood in there with him and helped him round, but for some reason he caught his hand, so after that anybody could have a go but he wouldn't go in with them!

Norman Gilburd

Norman and Phyllis Gilburd's wedding day.

Cheque-mate!

On Taro Fair day we used to have people coming round with a £5 note to pay for things – that was like a £50 note or more today – and they would say, 'I don't suppose you've got change for this, I'll take the stuff and just pop down the bank and get the change and be back.' All that sort of thing is rather like playing chess because they did catch me out now and then – but not very often.

Steve Pibworth

The old days...

We used to watch the fair being put up and in those days it stretched from the main gate of the Heath right out to the cricket pavilion. In our young days all the stalls were lit with paraffin flares; these were a sort of container with a long curved pipe with a spread burner, which made a rough sort of light with more smoke than flame.

You could have a ride on the roundabout or switchback, or take a donkey ride for ½d. On the morning of the fair there was the cattle and horse sale; it was fun watching and listening to the gypsies selling their ponies. We boys used to like to get up by the Red Lion tap room by the time the gypsies came out, half drunk, and watch the fights; women and all would join in and after someone had knocked out someone else's teeth they would all be calling one another 'dear brother' or 'sister'! It was an education!

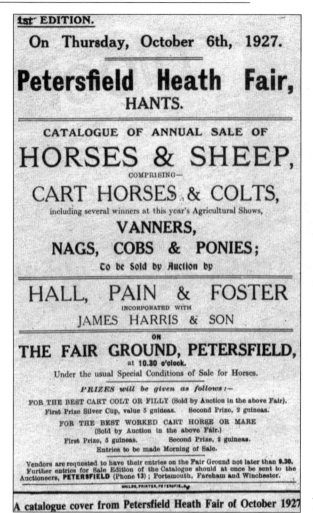

A *Petersfield Heath Fair catalogue cover from October 1927.*

People used to come from miles around – it was the one day of the year they met. Of course the fair still goes on but its all machines now; the old glamour has gone forever. It's a quarter the size it used to be, due, I think, to the toffee-nosed people living nearby who were influential with the council; if some of them had had their way it would be done away with altogether, but thank God they can't do that as it's a Charter to the Showman's Guild which goes back hundreds of years. I say long may it exist.

Harry Edwards

Above: '1928 Taro Fair' by Flora Twort.

Right: *Violet Sherrington and daughter Victoria (Jennifer Robinson's mother and sister) at the Taro Fair in 1944.*

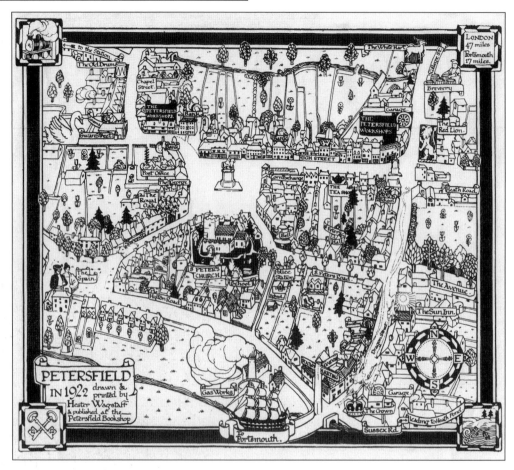

An illustrated map of Petersfield in 1922, drawn by Hester Wagstaff, a colleague of Flora Twort.